Ecology and the Environment

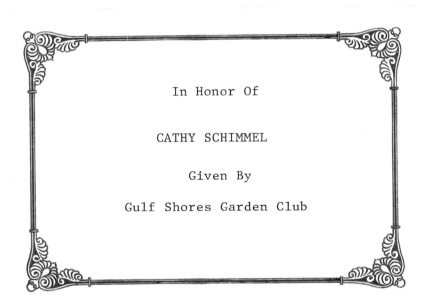

In Honor Of

CATHY SCHIMMEL

Given By

Gulf Shores Garden Club

Ecology and the Environment

A Look at Ecosystems of the World

Amy L. Tickle

Ann Arbor
THE UNIVERSITY OF MICHIGAN PRESS

Series Introduction

Content-based instruction (CBI) is the integration of content and language learning. **Alliance: The Michigan State University Textbook Series of Theme-based Content Instruction for ESL/EFL** is designed principally for postsecondary programs in English as a Second/Foreign Language, though some books are appropriate for secondary programs as well. **Alliance** is the first series to allow programs to experiment with content-based language instruction (CBI) without the demand of teachers' time and effort in developing materials. It also offers a wide selection of topics from which both teachers and students can choose.

The rationale for a content-based approach to language instruction comes from the claim that interesting and relevant material increases motivation and promotes effective language learning. CBI also adheres to the pedagogical principle that teaching should build on the previous subject matter *and* second language knowledge of the learner, while taking into account the eventual uses the learners will make of the second or foreign language. Finally, with a content-based approach, students will grow in not one but three areas: second language acquisition, content knowledge, and cognitive development.

Three models of CBI at the postsecondary levels exist: theme-based, sheltered, and adjunct. The **Alliance** series utilizes a theme-based approach in which language skills, grammar, vocabulary, and cognitive skills are integrated into the study of one particular subject area. This model is advantageous in that it can be implemented in any postsecondary program and can be taught at all proficiency levels. Sheltered and adjunct courses, on the other hand, are limited to university settings with high-intermediate to advanced level students. The theme-based approach is also preferable for this series as it is the only approach that has as its principal goal the improvement of language competence, rather than mastery of subject material.

Unique Features of the Series

All the textbooks have been piloted in the classroom by teachers other than the author. Because content-based instruction is a relatively new area of language teaching, our goal is to produce textbooks that are accessible to those teachers who have a great deal of experience with CBI and to those who have little or no experience. By piloting the textbooks with different teachers, we confirmed that people unfamiliar with the topic were able to teach the material easily. One teacher who taught the ecology text, said," I am an English teacher and I know next to nothing about the topic of ecology. As it turned out, the book gave me all the information that I needed." This piloting also allowed the author to receive feedback on which activities worked and didn't work, to determine whether or not the material was appropriate for the level, and to check for any "loopholes" in the textbook.

The teacher's manual provides detailed explanations for those who may want more guidance for teaching the course. Detailed explanations and information for teaching the materials are in the teacher's manuals. Teachers can use or not use the information, depending on their experience, needs and desire.

Each chapter in the student books states the content objectives, while teachers are provided with both content and language objectives in the teacher's manual. We expect that there is a range in teachers' philosophy toward CBI. Some teachers may accept wholly the idea that there should be no overt instruction of language, and that students will naturally acquire the language through the content. Some, however, may feel that overt language instruction is necessary. By restricting the language objectives to the teacher's manual, teachers have the option to share them with their students, or use them only as information to guide their teaching. The omission of the language objectives from the student's book also allows teachers to further develop any material and not feel obligated to cover "specified" language objectives.

Explanations of language items are clearly shown in "language boxes." Any detailed language point is explained in detail in "language boxes." These boxes give teachers the option to cover the material in class or to leave the information as reference for students to use on their own, depending on their philosophy toward CBI. The information in the language boxes also saves valuable time since teachers do not have to find the supporting language explanations from other textbooks.

Each book is devoted entirely to one particular content that builds on the students' previous learning experiences. This type of in-depth coverage allows topic-related vocabulary and concepts to be continuously recycled, thus increasing the students' knowledge of the content and language. Students will benefit from the coherence provided by an integrated skills approach with one unifying topical content.

The interest and needs of the learners are considered in the choice of topics. Our experience has shown that students have a wide variety of interests, some enjoying courses that are "entertainment" focused, such as music or film, while others prefer a more "academic" focus, such as American government or media. We have developed books that present different choices, and are immediately relevant to and useable in students' lives.

Several choices of topics exist for beginner, intermediate, and advanced level. As the student population varies from term to term, so will their needs and interests. Having more than one book to choose from at each level lets students choose the topic of special interest to them. Teachers can also choose topics they are comfortable with or interested in teaching.

Authentic materials are used whenever possible. One of the goals of CBI is to use original text that was created for a purpose other than language teaching. The structure, function, and discourse features in these materials then dictate what language is to be taught. While much of the information was kept in its original form, some of the authentic texts were adapted to match the language ability of the audience.

Content material is supplemented with activities that assist students in comprehension. The material in each book has been carefully analyzed to determine those language skills that will assist the students in comprehending the information. Activities have then been developed, along with any necessary language explanations to accomplish this goal.

Language items are presented in an inductive format. This format encourages students to generate for themselves how or why a particular form is used. This "active" discovery helps students retain the information more successfully.

Format of the Books

Each book in the Alliance series follow the same format, except in the Vocabulary Development section, present in some books but not in others. This format is as follows:

Opening Activity: Each chapter opens with some sort of activity that will get the students thinking about the topic of the chapter. This opening activity may be as simple as a picture, or may involve a detailed activity. Its purpose is not to master the content described, but simply to raise the students' awareness of the topic.

A Look Behind/A Look Ahead: This section contains a brief review of the previous chapter, and an overview of what the students will study in the current chapter.

To the Student: Each chapter lists the content objectives, and students are encouraged to read these before studying the chapter as a preview. They should also go over the objectives again at the end of the chapter to check for comprehension.

Vocabulary Development: Some of the texts include a section on vocabulary development so that the students have a list of the important chapter vocabulary words, as well as learn various strategies for developing that vocabulary.

Content Headings: The chapter is then divided into content areas marked with roman numerals. Within that content area, activities (labeled A, B, C, etc.) help students comprehend the material.

Series Acknowledgments

There are many people we need to thank for their help in making this series a reality. Most important, the authors deserve our gratitude for their dedication, insight, and cooperation toward the project despite their busy professional demands. We are also indebted to the entire staff at the English Language Center. Whether or not they were directly involved, everyone was willing to adjust schedules to accommodate and support the needs of the project. From our original meeting, Mary Erwin, our project editor has been our major supporter, urging, pushing, and cajoling us to meet deadlines. Her belief in this project has ultimately allowed these materials to see the light of day. Special thanks also goes to Peter Shaw of the Monterey Institute, who initially envisioned this project.

We are aware that there are still many theoretical and practical issues left to be resolved surrounding content-based instruction. We hope the Alliance Series will make some inroads toward the resolution of some of the issues, and lead to a better acceptance of this approach to language teaching in the field of ESL/EFL.

Susan Gass—Project Coordinator
Amy Tickle—Series Editor

Author Acknowledgments

The idea for not only this book but the series as well came from Peter Shaw and I thank him for the inspiration. Three teachers, Dave Farnworth, Anne Petti, and Cathy Fleck, piloted the course and gave me wonderful and insightful feedback. The reviewers also provided helpful suggestions for revision. Most importantly, I would like to thank Dr. Susan Gass, the director of the English Language Center, who gave me the incredible support I needed to complete this book. Danielle Steider, Patti Prince, Danielle Roy, and John Brinkerhuff, staff at the ELC, were also terrific in their help. Finally, a thanks to mom and dad; the knowledge needed to write this book came from your support.

Amy L. Tickle

Acknowledgments

Grateful acknowledgment is made to the following publishers, newspapers, magazines, and authors for permission to reprint copyrighted materials:

Aladdin Books for material from *Forests* by Dougal Dixon. London: 1984.

The Alaska Department of Environmental Conservation for the graphic *The Exxon Valdez.*

Aperture Foundation for material from *Vanishing Arctic: Alaska's National Wildlife Refuge* by T. H. Watkins. New York: 1988.

Chicago Tribune Company for material from "Greatest Oil Spill—How Terrible Was It?" by Casey Bukro. © Copyrighted (July 14, 1991) Chicago Tribune Company. All rights reserved. Used with permission.

Children's Press for material from *Hands on Ecology* by Ovid K. Wong. 1991.

Dover Publications for material from *Animals* by Jim Harter. New York: 1979.

Encyclopædia Britannica for "Deserts of the World." Adapted with permission from Encyclopædia Britannica, 15th edition. © 1988 by Encyclopædia Britannica, Inc.

Encyclopædia Britannica for The Foodchain in the Marine Environment, in the article titled "Biosphere." Reprinted with permission from Encyclopædia Britannica. © 1994 by Encyclopædia Britannica, Inc.

Grolier Incorporated for material from the *Academic American Encyclopedia,* 1994 edition. Copyright 1994 by Grolier Incorporated. Reprinted by permission.

Houghton Mifflin Company for material reproduced by permission from *The American Heritage Dictionary of the English Language.* 3d ed. Copyright 1992 by Houghton Mifflin Company.

John Plough for photographs used on the cover and used in chapter 1.

Population Reference Bureau for the figure entitled World population through history.

Rainforest Alliance for *Some Facts on Tropical Forests.* New York: 1993.

Wadsworth Publishing Company for material from *Living in the Environment* by G. Tyler Miller, Jr. © 1979 Wadsworth Publishing Company.

W. W. Norton & Company, Inc. for material reproduced from *An Introduction to Ecology and Population Biology* by Thomas C. Emmel, by permission of W. W. Norton & Company, Inc. Copyright © 1973 by W. W. Norton & Company, Inc.

To the Student

Welcome to *Ecology and the Environment: A Look at Ecosystems of the World.* By studying this book, you will improve your English and help with the goal of a healthier planet. First, you will learn some basic information about ecology, the study of the interaction of living and nonliving things. This study will help you better understand some of the environmental problems the world faces today. Then you will study several different ecosystems, or places in the world. For example, you will learn about the ecology of the forest, the ocean, the tundra, the grassland, and the desert, and how deforestation, oil spills, oil exploration, global warming, and desertification threaten life in these ecosystems and on the entire planet.

Contents

Chapter 1

An Introduction to Ecology and the Environment

Study the photograph assigned to your group. In the spaces, list all the words that come to mind as you study the picture. An example is provided to get you started. Here are some things to think about: plants, climate, human activities, animals, environmental consequences, etc.

Forest

Ocean
whale

Tundra

Grassland

Desert

To the Student

After completing this chapter, you will be able to

1. understand the parts of the biosphere.
2. define ecology and an ecosystem.
3. list the different types of ecosystems and their basic characteristics.
4. describe some current environmental problems and their causes.

After completing this chapter, return to this page and assess your own achievement in reaching these objectives.

Vocabulary Development

Learning the following words is important in order for you to understand this chapter. Go through this list and put a check next to the words you know. When you are finished with the chapter, return to this list and make sure you can put a check next to all of the words. There is also room to list any additional words you have learned.

__wildlife	__organic	__minerals
__animal	__plant	__species
__population	__community	__habitat
__ecology	__ecosystem	__biosphere
__environment	__biology	__physical
__organism	__tree	__regulate
__tundra	__grassland	__urban
__desert	__decompose	__atmosphere
__galaxy	__biotic	__abiotic

___ devastate   ___ hydrosphere   ___ lithosphere

___ technology   ___ deforestation   ___ catastrophe

___ abuse   ___ depletion   ___ precipitation

___ delicate   ___ biome   ___ terrestrial

_____   _____   _____

I. Geography Overview

A. Study the map of the world. Then read the following sentences. For each sentence put the number in the appropriate box on the map. The first sentence has been done for you.

1. The *Exxon Valdez* oil spill in Alaska on March 24, 1989 was 11 million gallons.
2. Tropical rain forests such as the Amazon in Brazil cover only 7% of the earth's surface, but they contain between 50–80% of the planet's species.
3. The Greenbelt Movement in Kenya has inspired women in rural villages to plant millions of young trees to prevent the spread of the desert.
4. India has been planting over three million acres of trees each year, but it is still losing forest because so many trees are cut for fuel, building materials, and agriculture.
5. Japan is the largest importer of tropical hardwood products.
6. Penguins in Antarctica are threatened with extinction because of development.
7. The average temperature over much of Russia is expected to rise 6 to 10°C because of global warming.
8. By the year 2000, half the people in the world will live in cities, and the largest city in the world will probably be Mexico City.

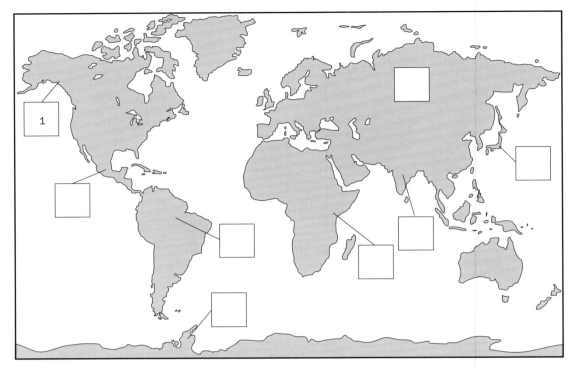

Map of the world

II. Exploration

A. In this activity, you will study outside of the classroom: work seriously and enjoy yourselves!

Form teams of three or four students and select a nearby area to explore. This area could be any of the following, depending on the location of your school:

a park   a river   a beach
a forest   a garden   a parking lot

Take with you the following items:

a sketchpad and pencils
a notebook and pen or pencil
a magnifying glass (optional)
a camera (optional)
an open mind

Your job is to make two lists: (1) all the living things you encounter in the area; (2) all the nonliving things. You can do this by:

writing lists
drawing a sketch of the area and marking items you see
making a map of the area
sketching or drawing items you cannot name
taking photographs

Do your best to leave the area as you found it. For example, if you lift a stone, replace it where you found it. Do not bring the item back to the classroom.

B. When you have identified everything, list the items in the following chart.

Living Things	Nonliving Things

III. About Ecology

A. Look at the title of the reading passage in Activity C. Based on this title, what do you predict this reading will be about? Write down any words or phrases in the space below that represent what the text will be about.

Predicting and Previewing

You have just used one reading skill: predicting. Another reading skill is previewing. Both of these skills give you enough information about the text so that you begin to think about it and form opinions about it. Then, when you do read the text, you can understand it better. Predicting and previewing help you to read more effectively.

B. Preview the text by reading it as quickly as possible. You can do this by reading the title and any headings, the first sentence of every paragraph, and all the tables and graphs. Then write down the vocabulary and the ideas that you remember.

C. Read the following passage.

ECOLOGY: THE UNDERSTANDING OF A DELICATE BALANCE

In recent years, there have been many natural catastrophes, such as forest fires in the western United States and floods in Bangladesh, as well as instances of environmental problems like oil spills and global warming. As a result of these events, more and more people are thinking about the environment. Many people believe that human activities cause these catastrophes and environmental problems. Indeed, since the Industrial Revolution, which began in the late 1800s, large increases in population and increased technology have led to significant changes to the surface of the earth and the atmosphere above.

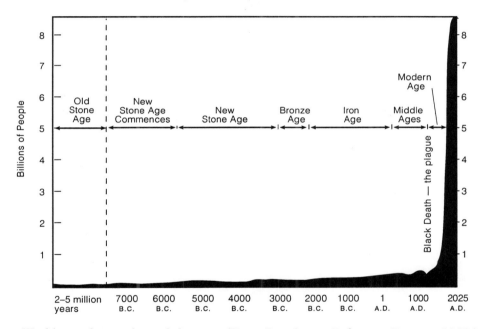

World population through history. (From Population Reference Bureau 1989.)

In order to solve these problems, we must understand the delicate balance that exists between living organisms and their environments. We can begin by looking at the biosphere.

THE BIOSPHERE

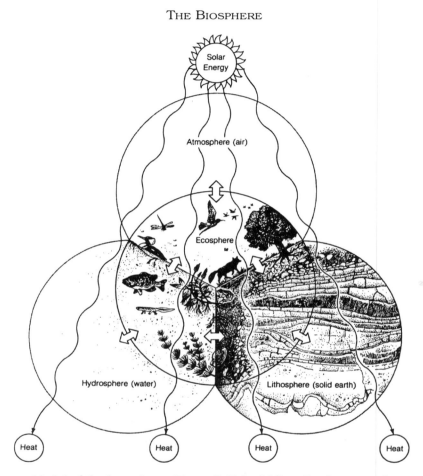

Model of the biosphere. (From G. Tyler Miller, Jr., *Living in the Environment* [Belmont, Calif.: Wadsworth, 1979].)

The *biosphere*, which allows life to exist on earth, is the thin layer of air (the *atmosphere*), water (*hydrosphere*), and soil and rock (*lithosphere*) that surrounds the planet. The biosphere includes any place on, above, below, or within the earth's surface where life can be found. The living part of the biosphere is called the *biotic component* and includes everything from plants to insects. The nonliving, or *abiotic component,* includes the physical characteristics of the biosphere, like soil, air, and water. The biosphere is regulated by the cycling of minerals and water between the abiotic and biotic components. Humans have an impact on this regulation.

The study of the biosphere is divided into several scientific disciplines, or areas of study. For example, *chemistry* is the science that studies subatomic particles, atoms, and molecules. *Biology* is concerned with protoplasm, cells, tissues, and organ systems. *Astronomy* is the science that studies planets, stars, galaxies, and the universe.

These disciplines are all important for understanding the planet we live on; however, in this book we are concerned with the study of *ecology*. Ecology is the study of how all living things interact with one another and their nonliving environment. The study of ecology is concerned with five levels: organisms, populations, communities, ecosystems, and the biosphere. *Organisms* are indi-

gray squirrel	organism
tree	habitat
all gray squirrels	population
squirrels, blue jays, deer, etc.	community
forest	ecosystem

vidual living things that belong to the same species. Organisms of the same species that live in the same geographic area are called *populations*. A *habitat* is the place where the organism or population lives. A *community* includes all the populations of organisms that live and interact with one another in a given area at a given time. When scientists use the term *ecosystem*, they are referring to the interactions between a particular community and its physical environment.

We can no longer ignore the effect humans have on the planet. Even changes in places far away affect us and our environment. Our actions today may decide the future of the planet. The study of ecology increases our understanding of planet earth. You are now taking the first important step toward positive change for a healthier planet.

D. Match the following vocabulary words from the passage to their correct definition.

global warming	oil spill	catastrophe	significant
technology	severe	delicate	regulate
impact	interaction	biotic	abiotic

1. _____ easily damaged

2. _____ important

3. _____ large amounts of oil in the ocean from an accident

4. _____ a great disaster

5. _____ to control or adjust

6. _____ the practical application of science

7. _____ nonliving

8. _____ the relationship between two things

9. _____ serious or violent

10. _____ the force of something

11. _____ the gradual warming of the earth's temperature

12. _____ living

E. Look at the following list. Using brackets, identify which groups of items are included in the four areas of scientific study. One group has been identified for you.

chemistry   biology   astronomy   ecology

other galaxies
our galaxy
stars
planets in the solar system
the planet earth
biosphere ⎫
ecosystem ⎪
community ⎬ ecology
population ⎪
organism ⎭
internal organs
tissues
cells
molecules
atoms
subatomic particles

F. Complete each sentence in the following paragraph with the appropriate word or phrase.

community   population   organism   ecosystem   habitat

An example of a(n) _____ is all the living and nonliving

components interacting in a given ocean. A school of dolphins is one

_____ that lives in the ocean. The school of dolphins, to-

gether with other fish, plants, and animals such as sea otters, forms

a(n) _____ . Each individual dolphin is called a(n)

_____ .

G. Answer the following questions about the reading.

1. Give at least two examples of a weather-related catastrophe.

2. Name two results of the Industrial Revolution.

3. Define the term *biosphere*.

IV. The Ecosystem

A. In this book, we will study ecology by looking at several different ecosystems. Write the definition for an ecosystem here.

ecosystem: _____

_____

An ecosystem can be a pond, a meadow, a forest, or the entire planet! An ecosystem may often contain smaller ecosystems. For example, in a forest, there may be a pond. Therefore, there are many ecosystems on the planet.

In order to make this less confusing, ecologists try to organize ecosystems into groups. The two major categories of ecosystems are *aquatic,* or areas with water such as an ocean or pond, and *terrestrial,* which are land ecosystems such as a forest or grassland. The terrestrial ecosystems are called *biomes,* and they are named for the vegetation (grass, plant, or tree) that grows there.

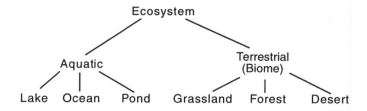

V. Overview to Ecosystems of the World

A. Look at the chart in Activity B. This chart lists several different ecosystems, such as a desert or tropical rain forest, and some biotic and abiotic features, such as soil and plants. Based on your own knowledge, fill in as much of the table as possible. Then, work with a partner to share your information.

B. Scan the following paragraph and fill in the chart with the appropriate information.

> The tropical rain forest occupies low-lying areas near the equator where the annual rainfall exceeds 80 to 90 inches. Rain is the only form of precipitation. There are usually one or more dry periods each year. This ecosystem contains the largest diversity of plant and animal life. A typical tree, such as a broadleaf evergreen tree, is tall, with many vines climbing its trunk, and a large canopy where animals live. A famous flower that grows here is called the rosy periwinkle. This flower is famous because it contains a cure for some types of cancer. Animals that are common in this ecosystem include monkeys and a colorful bird called the toucan. The soil, which is reddish in color and formed by rock decay, has a high concentration of iron and aluminum. The heavy rains, however, quickly wash these minerals from the soil.

Scanning

Another reading skill called *scanning* is used when you are looking for specific information in a reading. You do not read every word in the text; in fact, it is not important to understand every word in the text. All you want to do is find the necessary information. For example, think about when you read a newspaper in your native language. You might find an interesting article, but you probably don't read every word. Instead, you usually look for information such as when, how, or why something happened. Scanning is therefore done at a high speed.

	Characteristics of Ecosystems				
Ecosystem	Soil	Plant	Bird	Animal	Climate
Temperate deciduous forest					
Tropical rain forest					
Ocean					
Tundra					
Grassland					
Desert					

C. Listen carefully to the speaker and fill in the chart according to what you hear. You may take notes on a sheet of paper or write directly onto the chart. After the lecture is over, share the information you heard with a partner. Then listen again to check your answers.

D. Finish the chart by researching a particular ecosystem in the library. If you are presently living in one of these ecosystems, you can also go outside and record your observations, as well as interview local residents.

VI. An Introduction to Environmental Problems

In the reading earlier in this chapter, we learned that by studying ecology, we can help solve some of the serious environmental problems the world faces today.

A. Brainstorm a list of all the environmental problems that you know about.

Brainstorming

Brainstorming is a technique that helps people think of creative ideas. When people face problems, brainstorming is commonly used to help people think of new solutions. The rules for brainstorming are:

1. No ideas are ever criticized.
2. Unusual ideas are great!
3. The *quantity* of ideas is more important than the *quality*.
4. When one person shares an idea, the group should try to make suggestions to improve that idea. In other words, there are no stupid ideas! They can all be useful.

List of Current Environmental Problems in the World

B. Scientists agree that there are three main causes of environmental problems. These causes are:

population growth
abuse of natural resources
pollution

These causes are interrelated. In other words, one environmental problem may be caused by several things, and that is why these problems are difficult to solve.

The accompanying headlines about environmental problems are from newspapers and magazines. Read these headlines and decide what is the cause of the problem mentioned in the headline. Then fit all the headlines in the chart. What do you think these articles discuss?

Too Many Mouths

A Stinking Mess

Protecting Wildlife From Thoughtless Destruction: Are Your Daily Habits Deadly?

Is There Room For Anybody Else?

Oil Development and the Arctic National Wildlife Refuge

Beauty Endangered: Amazon Natives Seek Control of Their Land

A Billion More

Greatest Oil Spill

Global Climatic Change

Population Growth	Abuse of Natural Resources	Pollution

C. Add to the chart your list of environmental problems from Activity A.

Chapter 2

The Structure of
an Ecosystem

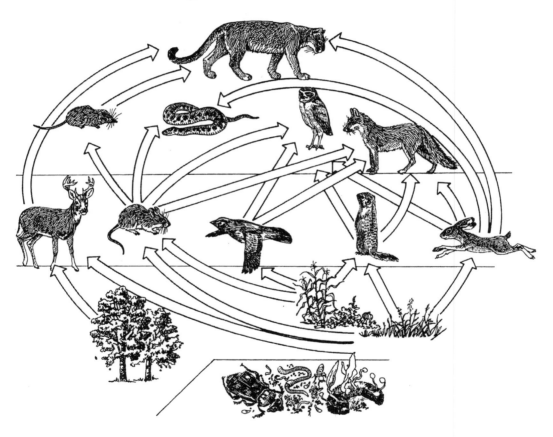

The food web. (From G. Tyler Miller, Jr., *Living in the Environment* [Belmont, Calif.: Wadsworth, 1979].)

In the picture on this page, can you identify. . . .

the largest source of energy
the primary consumer
the herbivore
the producer

An ecosystem. (From G. Tyler Miller, Jr., *Living in the Environment* [Belmont, Calif.: Wadsworth, 1979].)

A Look Behind/A Look Ahead

In chapter 1, we learned that ecology is the study of the interaction of living and nonliving things. Ecologists are concerned with the biosphere, which is where life exists. Within this biosphere, there are ecosystems, which are communities of organisms in a given area that interact with their nonliving environment.

Currently the world is facing many environmental problems, which are caused by population growth, abuse of natural resources, and pollution. It is important to understand ecology so we can begin to solve these global issues.

In this chapter, we will look at the structure of an ecosystem and how an ecosystem functions or works.

To the Student

After completing this chapter, you will be able to

1. describe the structure of an ecosystem.
2. state the abiotic components of an ecosystem.
3. understand basic chemical elements and formulae.
4. understand the concepts of energy and matter.
5. list various physical factors and describe how they affect the distribution of living things.
6. describe a typical food chain.
7. explain how energy flows through an ecosystem.
8. explain how materials cycle in an ecosystem.

After completing this chapter, return to this page and assess your own achievement in reaching these objectives.

Vocabulary Development

Words are divided into syllables, which are the basic unit of English pronunciation. Look at the following words and notice the different number of syllables in each.

1 syllable	2 syllables	3 syllables
gas	matter	elements

Learning the following words is important in order for you to understand this chapter. First, read the words out loud and decide how many syllables they have. Then put them in the appropriate place in the chart on page 21. One word has been added as an example. Next, go through this list and put a check next to the vocabulary words you know. When you are finished with the chapter, return to this list and make sure you can put a check next to all of the words. There is also room to list any additional words you have learned.

___ energy   ___ matter   ___ solid

___ liquid   ___ gas   ___ elements

___ atoms   ___ molecules   ___ photosynthesis

___ respiration   ___ food chain   ___ producer

___ consumer   ___ autotroph   ___ heterotroph

___ herbivores   ___ carnivores   ___ omnivores

___ decomposer   ___ nitrogen   ___ carbon

___ oxygen   ___ reservoir   ___ hydrological

___ evaporation   ___ condensation   ___ chlorophyll

_____   _____   _____

1 Syllable	2 Syllables	3 Syllables	4 Syllables	5 Syllables
		elements		

I. Defining the Structure of an Ecosystem

The structure of an ecosystem is determined by the abiotic and biotic components that can be found in that ecosystem.

A. Look at the picture on page 19. Write all of the things you can see in the picture in the following chart by deciding if they are biotic (living) or abiotic (nonliving).

Biotic	Abiotic

The *abiotic component* of an ecosystem consists of:

    energy
    matter (nutrients and chemicals)
    physical factors

B. In this same picture, where does the energy come from?

II. A Brief Look at Chemistry

Remember in chapter 1 we learned that chemistry is the study of molecules, atoms, and subatomic particles. A group of atoms of one kind makes a chemical element, and groups of *chemical elements* make *chemical compounds*. All matter is made up of chemical elements or compounds.

    Chemical elements have chemical symbols, and they appear in a chart called the periodic table. This chart is internationally understood; therefore, the symbol for a substance like *oxygen* will be represented by the letter *O* all over the world.

The Periodic Table of Elements

H Hydrogen																	He Helium
Li Lithium	Be Beyllium											B Boron	C Carbon	N Nitrogen	O Oxygen	F Fluorine	Ne Neon
Na Sodium	Mg Magnesium											Al Aluminum	Si Silicon	P Phosphorus	S Sulfur	Cl Chlorine	Ar Argon
K Potassium	Ca Calcium	Sc Scandium	Ti Titanium	V Vanadium	Cr Chromium	Mn Manganese	Fe Iron	Co Cobalt	Ni Nickel	Cu Copper	Zn Zink	Ga Gallium	Ge Germanium	As Arsenic	Se Selenium	Br Bromine	Kr Krypton
Rb Rubidium	Sr Strontium	Y Yttrium	Zr Zirconium	Nb Niobium	Mo Molybdenum	Tc Technetium	Ru Ruthenium	Rh Rhodium	Pd Palladium	Ag Silver	Cd Cadmium	In Indium	Sn Tin	Sb Antimony	Te Tellurium	I Iodine	Xe Xenon
Cs Cesium	Ba Barium	La Lanthanum	Hf Hafnium	Ta Tantalum	W Tungsten	Re Rhenium	Os Osmium	Ir Iridium	Pt Platinum	Au Gold	Hg Mercury	Tl Thallium	Pb Lead	Bi Bismuth	Po Polonium	At Astatine	Rn Radon
Fr Francium	Ra Radium	Ac Actinium	Rf Rutherfordium	Ha Hahnium													

Ce Cerium	Pr Praseodymium	Nd Neodymium	Pm Promethium	Sm Samarium	Eu Europium	Gd Gadolinium	Tb Terbium	Dy Dysprosium	Ho Holmium	Er Erbium	Tm Thulium	Yb Ytterbium	Lu Lutetium
Th Thorium	Pa Protactinium	U Uranium	Np Neptunium	Pu Plutonium	Am Americium	Cm Curium	Bk Berkelium	Cf Californium	Es Einsteinium	Fm Fermium	Md Mendelevium	No Nobelium	Lr Lawrencium

A. Match each chemical element to its correct chemical symbol. These elements and symbols will be used in this text, so it is important that you learn them.

Chemical Element   *Chemical Symbol*

___ Aluminum   O

___ Carbon   K

___ Chlorine   Zn

___ Copper   Al

___ Fluorine   N

___ Hydrogen   Na

___ Iron   Cl

___ Lead   C

___ Magnesium   F

___ Nitrogen   Pb

___ Oxygen   Fe

___ Phosphorous   Cu

___ Potassium   S

___ Sodium   P

___ Sulfur   Mg

___ Zinc   H

A *chemical compound* is a substance consisting of two or more elements chemically combined. Compounds have chemical formulas, which are a combination of the symbols for the elements in the compound.

Name of Chemical Compound	Chemical Formula	Elements
water	H_2O	hydrogen + oxygen
table salt	NaCl	sodium + chlorine

B. Below are the names of some chemical compounds and their formulas. Study this list as you will see these formulas again in this book.

SO_2 = sulfur dioxide H_2O = water $C_6H_{12}O_6$ = glucose sugar
CO_2 = carbon dioxide CH_4 = methane N_2O = nitrous oxide

III. Energy and Matter

A. Read sentences 1 to 10. Fill in the blank with either the word *energy* or *matter.* Sentence 5 has been completed as an example.

1. _____ is used for many purposes; for example, it is used to build shelters, to make food, and to keep our bodies alive.

2. These forms of _____ are solids (wood, iron, granite), liquids (water, petroleum), and gases (oxygen, hydrogen).

3. In other words, _____ is needed to move something from one place to another or to change it from one form to another.

4. They can be changed and moved from place to place, yet _____ is neither created nor destroyed in the process.

5. _Matter_ is the stuff that all things in this world are made of.

6. The biggest source of _____ for any ecosystem is the sun.

7. Everything on earth—animals, plants, rocks, soil, rivers, air—is composed of _____ .

8. _____ has three basic forms.

9. _____ is defined as the capacity to do some kind of work.

10. It cannot be recycled; therefore, the earth continuously receives and uses _____ from the sun.

Now we want to combine these sentences into two separate paragraphs on energy and matter. First, we must think about how paragraphs are organized in English.

Organization of Paragraphs

In English, paragraphs are usually written with the general idea first, followed by specific details which support the general idea.

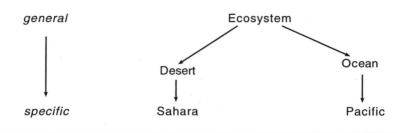

B. Arrange each of the following lists from general to specific. Write 1 for the most general, 2 for the choice in between, and 3 for the most specific.

Example:

solar system   1

earth   3

planets   2

1.   ecosystem   —

     Amazon   —

     rainforest   —

2.   rosy periwinkle   —

     plant   —

     flower   —

3.   matter   —

     liquid   —

     water   —

4.   hydrosphere   —

     biosphere   —

     ocean   —

C. Go back to the sentences about energy and matter in Activity A. Put the sentences about energy and matter in order. Use your knowledge of general to specific organization to help you. The first sentence in each paragraph is given to you.

1. Paragraph on energy

Energy is defined as the capacity to do some kind of work.

2. Paragraph on matter

Matter is the stuff that all things in this world are made of.

-

D. How did you know how to organize these paragraphs?

Cohesive Tools for Paragraphs

We have already learned that paragraphs are usually ordered from general to specific. There are also two tools in English that help writers organize paragraphs so that they are coherent: *repetition and substitution of key words,* and *logical connectors.*

Repetition and Substitution of Key Words

Matter has three basic *forms.* These *forms* are solids (wood, iron, granite), liquids (water, petroleum), and gases (oxygen, hydrogen).

Energy is used for many purposes; for example, *it* is used to build shelters, to make food, and to keep our bodies alive.

In the first example, the key word *form* has been repeated. In the second example, the pronoun *it* substitutes for the key word *energy.*

Logical Connectors

They can be changed and moved from place to place, *yet* matter is neither created nor destroyed in the process.

In this sentence, the logical connector *yet* shows a contrasting relationship between the first independent clause and the second independent clause. We will discuss logical connectors in more detail in the next section of this chapter.

E. Go back to your paragraphs in Activity C and underline all of the instances of repetition of key words. Then, circle all the logical connectors.

IV. Physical Factors

A. Look at the following pictures. Can the koala bear in the left picture live in the same place as the polar bear? Why or why not? What physical factors are different in each of their ecosystems?

B. Here is a list of some physical factors that determine what plants and animals can live in certain ecosystems. Can you rearrange the letters to solve the puzzle?

1. aeeemprrttu

2. ilos

3. iwdn

4. npatpeoriiict

5. ghilt

6. aceilmt

7. itseturnn

8. ymutihdi

C. In the accompanying short paragraph about physical factors, what sentence tells you the main idea of the paragraph?

The physical factors of an ecosystem are important abiotic characteristics. These physical factors, sometimes called *limiting factors*, are different for every ecosystem and determine what living things will exist in that ecosystem.

Topic Sentences

Earlier we learned that paragraphs in English usually begin with a general statement followed by specific details. The general statement at the beginning of a paragraph usually tells you the main idea of the paragraph. This sentence that states the main idea is called the *topic sentence.*

D. Match the topic sentences to their correct paragraphs about limiting factors.

Temperature can act as a limiting factor.
During the winter, some mammals become dormant, or *hibernate.*
Temperature may have a significant effect on the appearance of organisms.
Animals that maintain themselves at their optimum temperature are warm-blooded or homeothermic.

1. _____

_____ . At this time, the body temperature (normally about 100°F) falls to 45°F or even lower. The heart beat of a ground squirrel drops from a summer average of over 200 beats per minute to an average of less than 20 beats per minute in the winter.

2. _____

_____ . For example, the distribution of the polar bear is limited to regions in which the temperature averages no higher than 32°F. On the other hand, the malarial parasite does not develop when the temperature goes below 77°F.

3. _____

_____ . In other words, the weather outside can change, but they will keep the same temperature. If this temperature regulator doesn't work, however, the animal will die. If a person is kept in cold weather for too long, the temperature of his/her body will fall. When a person's body temperature falls to 65°F, the heart will fail.

4. _____

_____ . The Himalayan rabbit is mostly white but has black ears, tail, and feet. If the hair is taken from a white area, it will grow back white if the animal is kept at room temperature (68°F). However, if the animal is kept at a temperature below 50°F, the hair will grow back black.

E. Now see if you can write your own topic sentences for these paragraphs about ecosystems.

1. _____

_____ . For example, they both have long, cold winters. In addition, neither of these ecosystems has trees. The tundra has mostly low-lying plants, while the grassland has grasses.

2. _____

_____ . The biotic component consists of all the living things in the ecosystem. The abiotic component consists of energy, matter, and physical factors. Physical factors include things like precipitation, wind, and soil. All of these elements help determine what occurs in a particular ecosystem.

F. Go back to the paragraphs in activities D and E and underline all the logical connectors.

Logical Connectors

Logical connectors show a relationship between two sentences or clauses. There are two kinds of logical connectors: *coordinating conjunctions* and *conjunctive adverbs* (sometimes called *transition signals*).

Coordinating Conjunctions

Independent clauses can be combined using one of the seven coordinating conjunctions in English (*for, and, nor, but, or, yet, so*):

> A limiting factor for a polar bear is temperature, *so* they live in cold places.

Note that independent clauses can be joined by a semicolon to show that two ideas are very closely related. When you use a semicolon, do not use a coordinating conjunction.

> A limiting factor for a polar bear is temperature; they live in cold places.

Conjunctive Adverbs

Independent clauses can also be combined with a conjunctive adverb. Note the different methods of punctuation.

> A limiting factor for a polar bear is temperature. *Therefore*, they live in cold places.
> A limiting factor for a polar bear is temperature; *therefore*, they live in cold places.

This list shows some common conjunctive adverbs.

accordingly	for example	in other words	on the other hand
after all	for instance	instead	otherwise
also	further	likewise	similarly
anyway	furthermore	meanwhile	still
as a result	hence	moreover	subsequently
besides	however	nevertheless	then
certainly	in addition	next	thereafter
consequently	indeed	of course	therefore
even so	in fact		thus

G. There are four basic categories of logical connectors that show the relationship between two clauses. Using the coordinating conjunctions and conjunctive adverbs listed in the language box on logical connectors, fill in the chart below. An example of each has been given.

	Coordinating Conjunction	Conjunctive Adverb
Adversative (opposing)	but	
Additive		
Causative		
Sequential		next

H. Complete the following passage with appropriate logical connectors.

A substratum (a solid surface that an organism can attach or rest on) can be a limiting factor. _____ , off the northern coast of California, there are three areas where brown algae grow crowded together. The substratum is rocky, and there is a stalk (the long stem of a plant) that attaches to the rock. The algae attach themselves to the stalk _____ _____ they can float without being washed ashore.

_____ , a short distance away, the

substratum is muddy with no rock. _____

_____ , there are no algae at all. _____

_____ , a rocky substratum is a limiting factor for brown

algae.

I. Combine the following pairs of sentences into one sentence using a coordinating conjunction or a conjunctive adverb. Pay attention to your punctuation!

Example: Plants and animals vary widely in their range of tolerance to physical factors. White-tailed deer and deer mice are found in a wide range of climates.

Plants and animals vary widely in their range of tolerance to physical factors; for example, white-tailed deer and deer mice are found in a range of climates.

1. There is plenty of carbon dioxide, water, oxygen, and mineral salts in the deeper part of the ocean. Green plants cannot grow there because of the absence of light.

2. In winter, honeybees gather together closely and vibrate their heavy wing muscles. They make enough heat to raise the temperature of the hive.

3. Light affects animals indirectly because animals depend on plants for their food. Light affects animals directly because it helps them to see their enemies.

4. Animals that live in a cave must leave the cave to feed. They must make the best of the food that is brought in.

V. Experiment on Limiting Factors

DOES PRECIPITATION AFFECT A BIRD POPULATION?

Objective

Analyze data to find the effect of precipitation on the hatching of eggs by sandhill
cranes, one of the tallest North American
birds.

Materials

calculator

Procedure

A. The following table shows the number of sandhill crane eggs hatched in the wild during an eight-year experiment. The amount of rainfall and snowfall during each of the eight years was also recorded. Study the data.

TABLE 1.   Sandhill Crane Eggs Hatched

Year	Number of Adults	Number of Nests	Number of Eggs Laid	Number of Eggs Hatched	Rainfall (cm)	Snowfall (cm)
1984	21	5	5	3	1.4	1.4
1985	23	3	5	1	2.5	5.5
1986	32	0	0	0	7.8	3.0
1987	26	11	11	8	3.2	0.7
1988	32	11	11	7	2.8	1.0
1989	30	5	5	4	3.5	0.5
1990	32	6	6	5	2.1	0.6
1991	30	4	6	1	6.4	2.4

B. Fill in the correct information in the table below using the data from table 1. Determine the total precipitation in each year by adding the amount of rainfall and snowfall. Find the percentage of eggs hatched in each year. To do this, divide the number of eggs hatched by the number of eggs laid, and then multiply by 100.

Year	Number of Eggs Laid	Number of Eggs Hatched	Rainfall (cm)	Snowfall (cm)	Total Precipitation (cm)	Percentage of Eggs Hatched

C. Using your data from Activity B, fill in the graph below to show how the amount of precipitation relates to the percentage of eggs hatched.

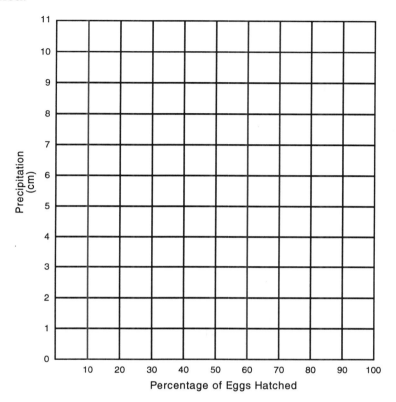

Results and Conclusions

D. Answer the following questions based on your data.

1. In which year was the precipitation lowest? Highest?

2. What seems to be the relationship between the amount of precipitation and the number of eggs hatched? Explain your answer.

3. On the basis of the data, does precipitation seem to be a limiting factor for the sandhill crane population? Explain your answer.

4. Does the effect of precipitation on the population seem to be dependent upon the density of the population? Explain your answer.

E. Write a paragraph summarizing the results of this experiment. Use the writing tools you have learned about in this chapter.

VI. The Food Chain and Energy

We learned earlier that the sun is the main source of energy for an ecosystem. In order to understand how an ecosystem works, we must understand the biotic component of an ecosystem, and how energy and materials move through it.

A. On this picture, draw an arrow to the place where the primary source of energy is used first.

B. Now you will hear a lecture about food chains that contains the following vocabulary words. When you hear these words, put them in the correct blank spaces in the following text.

autotroph	decomposer	herbivore
heterotroph	omnivore	producer
consumer	bacteria	carnivore

The food chain begins with green plants because they are able to use the sun's energy, along with carbon dioxide and water, to make food through photosynthesis. _____

_____—the plants that form the bottom, or base, of the food chain—are also called _____ because they can make their own food.

The higher levels are all _____ , which

are animals that cannot produce their own food. Instead, they

must obtain energy from other living organisms or from the dead

remains of plants and animals. These animals are also called

_____ , which can be divided into four

categories.

_____ are animals that eat only

plants. The second level of the food chain is made up of

_____ , which feed on _____

_____ . The top _____ in a food

chain feeds on other _____ . Animals that

eat both plants and animals are called _____

_____ . Therefore, they can be found at any level above

herbivores in a food chain. Finally, _____

are tiny organisms such as _____ that

break down dead plant and animal matter. This process releases

chemicals that the _____ can use again.

Thus, energy and matter is cycled through the ecosystem.

C. Fill in the missing parts of the diagram below, which summarizes
the biotic components of an ecosystem. Use the vocabulary words
on page 39 to complete the diagram.

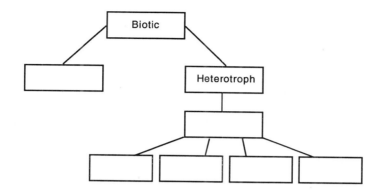

D. Now let's look at the picture on page 39 again. Use the vocabulary words to complete the following paragraph.

The first arrow goes from the sun to green plants, which are

called _____ , or _____

_____ . The second arrow goes from green plants to the

rabbit. This animal is called a _____

because it feeds on green plants. The next arrow should go from

this rabbit to the _____ . This animal is

called a _____ because it feeds on

_____ . An arrow should go from the

plants and animals that will die to the _____

_____ . These tiny organisms are called _____

_____ .

E. Look at the food chain represented as a pyramid. Fill in all the animals that you can think of for each of the levels. Note that an omnivore can appear on more than one level.

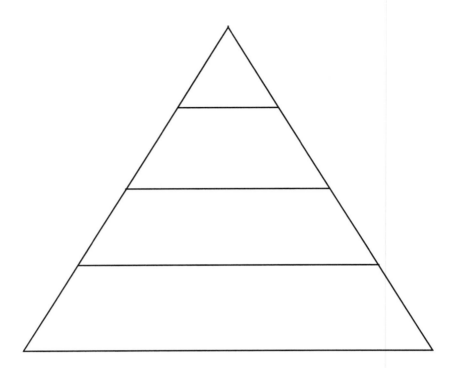

F. We can understand how energy is transferred by looking at the food chain as an energy pyramid. Like all food chains, the bottom of the pyramid is made up of producers. The other levels of the pyramid are made up of consumers.

Look at the figure and answer the following questions:

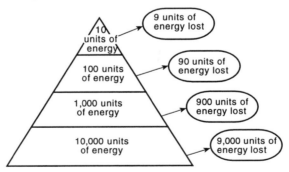

1. Where is the greatest amount of energy in the pyramid?

2. What percentage of the available energy is lost at each level of the food chain? How much available energy does this leave for the next level?

3. What do you think leads to this energy loss?

G. What does all of this mean? Our discussion leads us to two important ecological principles. In groups, discuss how these principles can be applied to current environmental problems. An example is provided for each principle.

All life and all forms of food begin with sunlight and green plants.
    If we cut forests we lose plants.

A shorter food chain uses food energy more efficiently.
    We need all the food energy possible to feed the growing number of people.

VII. How Materials Cycle in an Ecosystem

As we learned earlier, matter is the stuff that all things are made of. Matter is composed of certain chemical elements and compounds. We will look at how matter is transported through three important cycles: water, nitrogen, and carbon dioxide.

A. Listen to the lecture about the *hydrological cycle*. Write each of the following words in the appropriate arrow drawn in the diagram.

evaporation   condensation   absorption
precipitation   runoff

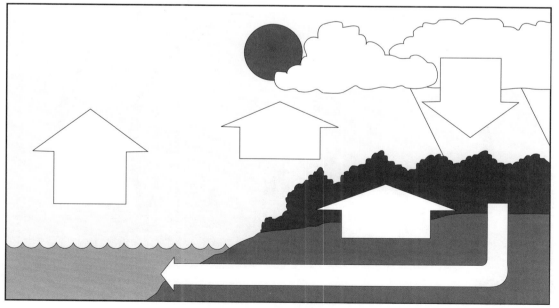

The water cycle. (From Dougal Dixon, *Forests* [London: Franklin Watts, 1984].)

B. Read the following paragraphs on the *nitrogen cycle.* Some of the sentences have numbers after them. Write that number in the corresponding box in the picture below.

Almost 80% of the air is nitrogen gas. But most living things cannot use nitrogen in this form. It must first be changed into nitrogen compounds. The process whereby nitrogen gas is changed into nitrogen compounds is called *nitrogen fixation.* The nitrogen cycle is the movement of nitrogen through an ecosystem.

There are two ways that nitrogen is *fixed* (changed from nitrogen gas to nitrogen compounds). The first is through lightning. As lightning passes through the air, it causes nitrogen to combine with oxygen to form nitrates (1). These compounds are washed out of the air to the earth by rain. Then plants and animals can use nitrogen in this form.

The second way that nitrogen can be *fixed* is by the actions of certain microorganisms called blue-green bacteria (2). After the nitrogen has been fixed, plants use this form of nitrogen (3). Then, animals eat the plants (4). When the animals die, the nitrogen in their bodies returns to the soil (5).

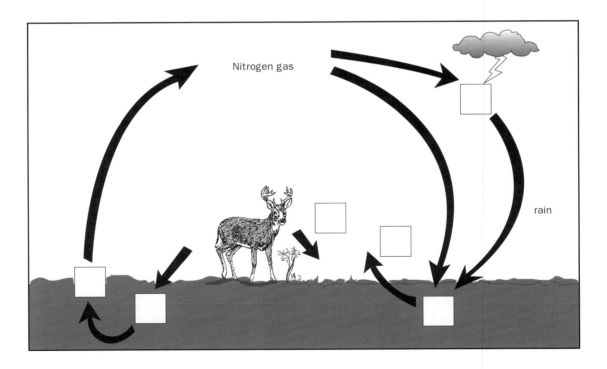

In order to complete the cycle, there has to be some nitrogen gas returned to the air so the process can start again. This is done by *denitrifying bacteria* (6). These bacteria live in the soil and change nitrogen compounds back into nitrogen gas.

C. Now read the following passage about the *carbon and oxygen cycle.* Then draw a chart which illustrates this passage.

The movement of carbon dioxide and oxygen through an ecosystem is called the carbon and oxygen cycle. In this passage, we will focus on the cycle of carbon dioxide. There are two ways that carbon dioxide is removed from the atmosphere. The first is through the ocean, which is like a huge reservoir that absorbs much of the gas. The second way is by plants that take in carbon dioxide through the process of photosynthesis.

In a natural system, carbon dioxide is released back into the atmosphere through *respiration* when an animal, such as a deer, breaks down food and energy is released. Carbon dioxide is also put back into the atmosphere through a process called *decomposition.* This process occurs when dead plants and animals are broken down by the actions of bacteria.

Human activity, however, has seriously affected this cycle by releasing more carbon dioxide into the atmosphere than is taken away. This extra carbon dioxide is released into the atmosphere in two ways. The first is through the burning of fossil fuels, such as coal, oil, and gas. The second is through *deforestation,* where trees are either cut or burned, releasing all the stored carbon dioxide into the air.

Chapter 3

The Forest Ecosystem

How many trees and animals of the forest ecosystem do you know? Match the names of these typical trees and animals from the forest ecosystem to their pictures.

Animals

__ snake	__ deer	__ raccoon	__ fox	__ owl
__ bear	__ squirrel	__ rabbit	__ toucan	__ beaver
__ moose	__ wolf	__ monkey	__ skunk	

Trees

__ oak   __ fir   __ maple   __ spruce

a.

b.

c.

d.

e.

f.

g.

h.

i.

j.

k.

l.

m.

n.

o.

p.

q.

r.

A Look Behind/A Look Ahead

In chapter 2, we learned about the structure of an ecosystem, which consists of biotic and abiotic components. In this chapter, we will look at the forest ecosystem, which is made up of three separate ecosystems: the *tropical rain forest*, the *temperate deciduous forest*, and the *taiga*, or northern coniferous forest. Using examples from these ecosystems, we will learn about the ecological concept of a *niche*. Finally, we will apply this knowledge to one environmental problem: *deforestation.*

To the Student

After completing this chapter, you will be able to

1. differentiate between broadleaf trees and needleleaf trees.
2. identify and describe the typical biotic and abiotic features of three forest ecosystems.
3. understand the concept of a niche.
4. describe the causes and effects of, and propose solutions to, deforestation.

After completing this chapter, return to this page and assess your own achievement in reaching these objectives.

Vocabulary Development

When words in English have more than one syllable, the word is pronounced with stress on one of the syllables. In the following word, there are three syllables, and the stress is on the second syllable.

com · mér · cial

Listen to your teacher pronounce each word in the vocabulary list for this chapter and mark the syllable that has the stress. Then go through the list and put a check next to the words you know. When you are finished with the chapter, return to this list and make sure you can put a check next to all of the words. There is also room to list any additional words you have learned.

___ broadleaf tree

___ remote

___ contrast

___ import

___ plan

___ maintain

___ peer review

___ pharmaceutical

___ coniferous

___ diversity

___ scavenger

___ elevation

___ needleleaf tree

___ equator

___ draft

___ commercial

___ feedback

___ albedo

___ temperate

___ interdependence

___ decomposition

___ deforestation

___ indigenous

___ extreme

___ compare

___ moisture

___ revise

___ complex

___ taiga

___ disrupt

___ niche

___ severe

___ hoof

___ parasite

___ organic

_____   _____   _____

I. Broadleaf and Needleleaf Trees

Two types of trees in the forest ecosystem are *broadleaf,* or deciduous, and *needleleaf,* or evergreen, *trees.* Look at the chart that describes these two types of trees.

	Broadleaf Trees	*Needleleaf Trees*
Kinds of trees	ash, elm, maple, wal-nut,oak	fir, pine, spruce
Leaves	broad and flat fall off the tree in autumn	narrow, pointed, needlelike permanent
Wood type	hardwood—tough, hard wood that is good for mak-ing furniture	softwood
Seeds	flowers develop into fruits that completely surround seeds	seeds are not enclosed; they lie openly on cones

A. Now we are going to prepare to write a short paragraph about these two types of trees. There are two ways to organize the information in a paper that compares (how are they alike?) and/or contrasts (how are they different?) two things.

1. Will your paragraph compare or contrast these two types of trees?

2. Turn back to chapter 2 and write down some logical connectors that will help you.

Comparison/Contrast Paragraphs

There are two main ways you can organize your paragraph: *subject-by-subject* or *point-by-point*. In *subject-by-subject* organization, you discuss one subject (broadleaf trees) and then the other subject (needleleaf trees), covering the same points (kinds of trees, leaves, wood, and seeds) *in the same order.*

> Broadleaf Trees
> > Kinds of Trees
> > Leaves
> > Wood
> > Seeds
>
> Needleleaf Trees
> > Kinds of Trees
> > Leaves
> > Wood
> > Seeds

In *point-by-point* organization, you discuss each point, moving back and forth between the two subjects.

> Kinds of Trees
> > Broadleaf
> > Needleleaf
>
> Leaves
> > Broadleaf
> > Needleleaf
>
> Wood
> > Broadleaf
> > Needleleaf
>
> Seeds
> > Broadleaf
> > Needleleaf

B. Take a few minutes to plan your paragraph about broadleaf and needleleaf trees. (We have already done some of this step by listing logical connectors and discussing organizational patterns.) Then write a draft on a separate sheet of paper. When you are finished, revise it.

The Writing Process and Peer Review

When people write, they usually don't sit down immediately and write from start to finish. Instead, most writers go through three stages: *planning, drafting,* and *revising.* Planning is the stage where you don't do any formal writing; instead, you may sit and think, visit the library, or talk to people about what you are going to write. The purpose of drafting is to get your ideas on paper without worrying about the organization or grammar. Revision is the stage where you concentrate on these points.

Writers, however, do not usually go through these steps or stages in order; they may plan for a while, write a draft, go back to planning, write a second draft, revise it, make a third draft, revise that, etc.

When you are revising, it sometimes helps to get *feedback* from other people. Usually, it is your teacher that does that. Often, however, people ask their coworkers or their classmates to make comments about their writing. This process is called *peer review.*

Although your classmates are learning English as a second language, too, there are many things you can learn from this process. First, peer reviewers can tell you whether or not they understand what you wrote. Second, you might learn about a different way to write when you read another person's paper. Finally, you will develop your skills at giving suggestions and receiving them from other people.

C. Exchange papers with another person in the class. Read the paper carefully, and complete the following worksheet. Then discuss the answers with your peer review partner.

My Name: _____ Writer's Name: _____

1. What organizational pattern does the writer use? subject-by-subject? point-by-point?

2. Is there anything the writer needs to add to the paper? Is there anything the writer needs to take out?

3. Do you have any other suggestions for the writer?

Now write another draft and submit this revised draft to your teacher.

II. The Forest Ecosystem

There are three main forest ecosystems: the *tropical rain forest*, the *temperate deciduous forest*, and the *taiga*. In Activity B we will learn more about these ecosystems, but, first, let's practice some vocabulary.

A. The vocabulary words numbered 1–9 appear in Activity B. Write the opposite meaning for each vocabulary word from the following choices and then write a definition for the vocabulary word.

inorganic	mild	build up	depth
same	average	near	without hooves
the poles	dryness		

Example:

organic
opposite: <u>inorganic</u>

definition: <u>something related to or derived from living organisms</u>

1. *decompose*
    opposite: _____

    definition: _____

2. *diversity*
    opposite: _____

    definition: _____

3. *elevation*

   opposite: _____

   definition: _____

4. *extreme*

   opposite: _____

   definition: _____

5. *severe*

   opposite: _____

   definition: _____

6. *hoofed*

   opposite: _____

   definition: _____

7. *remote*

   opposite: _____

   definition: _____

8. *equator*

   opposite: _____

   definition: _____

9. *moisture*

   opposite: _____

   definition: _____

B. In groups, read the information your teacher will give you and then fill in the following chart. After you have filled in your chart, you will have to visit the other groups to "teach" them about your ecosystem. You will also have to listen to them to get the information about the other ecosystems.

	Temperate Deciduous Forest	Taiga	Tropical Rain Forest
Location			
Climate (season, precipitation, temperature)			
Soil			
Typical Animals			

C. Based on the information you learned from your classmates, fill in the key to the following map about the three forest ecosystems.

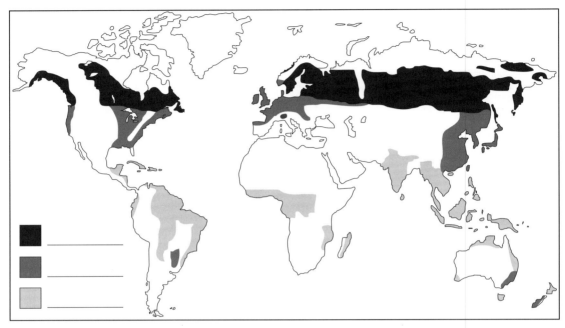

Distribution of forest types. (From Dougal Dixon, *Forests*. [London: Franklin Watts, 1984].)

D. Mark the following statements *true* or *false* based on the information in your chart from Activity B.

___ 1. Wolves live in the taiga.

___ 2. The taiga is the warmest forest ecosystem.

___ 3. The leaves on the trees in the taiga fall in autumn.

___ 4. Decomposition is fastest in the temperate deciduous forest.

___ 5. The temperate deciduous forest is colder than the taiga.

___ 6. The greatest diversity in plant and animal life is in the tropical rain forest.

E. Draw a food chain for each ecosystem on a separate piece of paper. You will need to ask the other groups for any information they have about the animals in their readings (or visit the library to see what these animals eat).

III. What Is a Niche?

A. You will hear a lecture on the ecological concept of a *niche*. Before you hear the lecture, briefly discuss the following questions.

1. Do you have a job? What jobs have you had in the past?
2. What are some typical jobs in the community that you live in now?
3. Do animals have jobs? What jobs do they have?

Taking Lecture Notes—Using Abbreviations

There are many situations you may find yourself in where you want to take notes on a talk you are listening to. The challenge in taking notes is to: (1) try to understand the organization of the talk in order to organize your notes; (2) identify the important details; and (3) write fast enough to record these details. This is a difficult job in a first language, but even more so in a second language. Therefore, it is important that you be patient and understand that note taking is a skill that requires a lot of practice.

To help take notes more quickly, you can use several note-taking symbols and abbreviations. There are no rules for how to abbreviate words (make them shorter) when you are taking notes. People all abbreviate words a little differently.

There are three things to think about when you abbreviate words. First, once you have decided on an abbreviation, you should be consistent, so that you know what the abbreviation means when you look at your notes later. Second, be careful how you abbreviate words, so that they can't be confused with another word. For example:

abbreviation = *ind.*

This abbreviation could mean *ind*ependent, *ind*ecisive, *ind*ecision, or many other words. Finally, when you learn new terms, you should spell out the term when it is first used and then abbreviate it for the remainder of your notes. For example, if you hear a talk that mentions the United Nations Population Fund, you would want to spell this out the first time, and then you could abbreviate it as UNPF in the rest of your notes.

B. Match the symbols on the left with their meanings. Write the appropriate letter in each blank.

___ =	___ ∴	a. therefore	g. less than
___ >	___ ↑	b. change	h. with
___ <	___ e.g.	c. approximately	i. equals
___ &	___ Δ	d. increase	j. more than
___ w/	___ ↓	e. for example	k. and
___ w/o	___ ≈	f. without	l. decrease

C. Rewrite the following passage using abbreviations and note-taking symbols.

Logging is only one cause of deforestation, but in Southeast Asia, it is an important one. And Japan is the world's largest consumer of tropical timber: in 1986 it imported 15.7 million cubic meters, approximately equal to the imports of the entire European community. (Eugene Linden, "Putting the Heat on Japan," *Time*, July 10, 1989, 51)

D. Listen to the opening of the lecture on niches and answer the following questions.

1. This lecture will be about . . .
   a. the structure of an ecosystem.
   b. the interaction between living things and their non-living environment.
   c. the structure of a community.

2. What words did the speaker use that helped you answer this question?

Taking Lecture Notes—Listening for Organization

There are many language clues you can listen for that will help you understand the organization of a talk. Understanding the organization will help you make predictions about what the person will say and will also help you to remember the information better.

In future chapters, we will continue to look at some of these language clues. For this particular lecture, listen for the language the speaker uses in the introduction to tell what the lecture is about.

Some lecturers state their goals very clearly with phrases such as "Today I will talk about *X*," or "I'd like to cover three goals." Other speakers may not state their purposes very clearly. As a listener, you generally should not worry about taking notes during the introduction. Instead, listen carefully to see if you can understand the purpose and organization of the entire talk.

E. Now listen to the lecture and take notes using the guide provided.

LECTURE ON NICHE

Human community-

  elements:

  jobs:

Niche = _____

  e.g.,

Niche—defn:

  a.

  b.

  c.

  d.

e. where, when, how it reproduces

f.

g.

F. The following list names many of the common niches in a biotic community. Match each niche to its description.

a. food producers   e. parasites
b. herbivores   f. scavengers
c. first-level carnivores   g. decomposers
d. second-level carnivores

__ These organisms feed on primary carnivores and are larger than their prey.

__ Their job is to turn plants into animal fat that can be used by animals higher up in the food chain. They are the most numerous of all animals, because it takes many of them to keep one carnivore going.

__ These animals eat dead plants or animals. Their job is to clean up the environment and to circulate dead material back into the living world.

__ These absorb the sun's energy and use it, together with water, carbon dioxide, and minerals, to manufacture carbohydrates, fats, proteins, vitamins, and other substances that provide energy.

__ These are mostly microorganisms. They break down the bodies of organisms into simple substances. The work of these organisms also releases carbon dioxide from dead plant and animal tissues, which can be reused by plants.

__ These animals feed on herbivores and vary in size. They are generally larger and stronger than their prey.

__ They get their energy by living off of other living organisms, usually without killing them.

IV. Environmental Application: Deforestation

A. In groups, brainstorm everything you know about deforestation. Write all these words, phrases, and sentences below.

B. Read the following statements about deforestation and decide if each statement describes a cause, an effect, or a solution. Write either the letter *C* for cause, *E* for effect, or *S* for solution in the blank spaces.

___ 1. The indigenous, or native, people will lose their traditions and ways of life.
___ 2. Tropical rain forests could be set aside as forest preserves.
___ 3. Japan is the largest importer of tropical hardwood products.
___ 4. Ben and Jerry's Homemade Ice Cream uses nonwood resources from the rain forest, like fruits and nuts, that can be used for a profit.
___ 5. The development of large industrial projects, such as hydroelectric dams or mines, have economic advantages, but these advantages may not be greater than the environmental damage.
___ 6. The rosy periwinkle, a flower found only in the rain forest, is disappearing. This flower contains a cure for Hodgkins disease (a type of cancer) and childhood leukemia.

C. These words or phrases come from the reading about deforestation on page 62. Match each one to its definition by writing the correct letter in the blank space.

___ 1. import
___ 2. lush
___ 3. global cooperation

___ 4. disrupt
___ 5. albedo

a. reflection of sunlight
b. to keep the same
c. bring things into a country
d. unbelievable, amazing
e. identified and named

—	6.	maintain	f. for profit
—	7.	complex	g. abundance of vegetation
—	8.	scientifically categorized	h. complicated, having many parts
—	9.	commercial	i. people of the world working together
—	10.	incredible	j. to change

D. Read the following article about deforestation. Ignore the stars (*) in the article for now. We will work with these in Activity F.

DEFORESTATION IN THE TROPICAL RAIN FORESTS

Tropical rain forests are the oldest and most diverse ecosystems on earth.* Green, lush, and full of life, rain forests are as mysterious and beautiful as they are important. Long before these mysteries are solved, however, rain forests may be gone.* Because of their importance to everyone on this planet, global cooperation and understanding are needed to solve this problem.

Tropical rain forests are *complex*, or complicated, ecosystems with incredible biotic diversity that is maintained by the perfect growing conditions of year-round heat and humidity. This high diversity means high *interdependence*. In other words, animals and plants depend on each other, which makes this ecosystem *vulnerable* to disturbance. For example, if hunters kill all the members of a bird species that pollinates a tree, the tree species will also die, and all the insects and animals that depend on that tree will die. Thus, it is easy to lose many species, and perhaps the entire ecosystem, with only a little disturbance.

The loss of plant and animal species in the rain forest means the loss of the important products we receive from the rain forest.*

Perhaps most valuable of all rain forest products are the many *pharmaceuticals*, or medicines, that have been made from forest plants. ** Much of the rain forest's plant and animal life has never been scientifically categorized, and scientists are concerned that valuable plants may be gone before they are ever studied.

Plants and animals are not the only important living things in a rain forest; there are also hundreds of thousands of *indigenous*, or native, people. These groups have developed ways to live in harmony with their environment, creating a stable balance between their needs and the needs of the forest. In addition, they hold the knowledge of their cultural traditions and ways of life, including important information on how to use the rain forest plants to treat disease.

A third, and perhaps the most important, reason to preserve the rain forest is the role that these forests play in creating and maintaining the environmental conditions that make human life possible.*

We know that rain forests are important, so why are they disappearing? *Commercial logging* is used to produce timber, paper pulp, and other wood products, and helps the countries make payments on foreign debts.** Another reason the rain forests are destroyed is to make way for the development of large *industrial projects*, such as hydroelectric dams or mines, which do have economic advantages, but these advantages may not be greater than the environmental damage. Finally, forests are also destroyed by farming. *Commercial agriculture,* which includes raising cattle for fast-food restaurants, destroys large amounts of tropical rain forests.

Tropical rain forests provide humanity with food, pharmaceuticals, building materials, and other products. Deforestation leads to the loss of these economy-sustaining export products, the loss of indigenous culture, and the disruption of climate. It must be slowed down or stopped.

E. Of these two sentences about deforestation, which is easier to understand and more convincing? Why?

Deforestation is a serious problem. Every year a lot of the tropical rain forest disappears.

Deforestation is a serious problem. Every minute eighty acres of tropical forest are destroyed.

Supporting Details

We learned in chapter 2 that most writing in English is organized from the general to the specific. In a paragraph, the most general statement is usually the topic sentence. The topic sentence is followed by specific statements, which are called *supporting details*. Supporting details are very important to good writing, because they help the reader understand your main point more easily, and they help convince the reader of the point you are making. Supporting details can be facts or statistics, examples, personal experiences, observations, or statements by authorities on the subject.

F. The following facts are all specific details about deforestation. Go back to the reading passage. Every place there is a star (*), a supporting detail is needed. If there is one star, choose one of the sentences; if there are two, choose two; etc. All of the information from the fact sheet should be used in the article.

SOME FACTS ON TROPICAL FORESTS

- Eighty acres of tropical forest are destroyed every minute.
- Tropical rain forests cover only two percent of the globe, yet contain half of the world's 5–10 million species, most of which have never been studied.
- We use tropical rain forest products whenever we read a book, drive a car, drink coffee, use deodorant, eat chocolate, or take medicine.
- More than one-quarter of the medicines prescribed in the United States come mostly from plants from the tropical rain forest.
- Seventy percent of the plants identified as having anticancer properties are found in tropical rain forests. For example, the rosy periwinkle is a rain forest flower that contains a cure for Hodgkin's disease (a type of cancer) and childhood leukemia.
- Because wood is the primary energy source for millions of people, collecting fuelwood destroys five million acres of tropical rain forests every year.
- Japan is the largest importer of tropical hardwood products, and the United States is second. Southeast Asia supplies most of these products. Although loggers may only select one tree out of twenty, up to two-thirds of the trees in that area are damaged by taking away the one tree.
- The loss of water-regulating influences, an increased *albedo* (reflection of sunlight), and the release of large amounts of carbon dioxide when trees are cut will lead to a disruption in the climate.

Adapted from "Some Facts on Tropical Forests," *Rainforest Alliance*, March, 1993.

G. Look at the following sentence. Based on the information in the sentence, can you write a definition of the word *indigenous*? What clues did you use to do this?

There are also hundreds of thousands of *indigenous*, or native, people.

Finding Definitions in a Text

Many times when you read something the writer will provide a definition for certain vocabulary words by using clue words or phrases. Look at the following examples.

Ecology *is* the study of the interaction between living and nonliving things.

Ecology, *or* the study of the interaction between living and nonliving things, is an important discipline for understanding our environment.

Ecology (the study of the interaction between living and nonliving things) is an important discipline for understanding our environment.

In the first example, the word *ecology* is defined by using the simple present tense of the verb *be*. In the second example, the language clue used to define ecology is the connector *or*, and the definition, all enclosed in commas. A writer can also enclose definitions in parentheses or dashes, as in the third example.

Sometimes, the word is not clearly defined, but the writer provides an example that helps you make an intelligent guess about the meaning.

Carnivores, *such as* lions, tigers, and wolves, are usually larger than their prey.

In this sentence the writer has given the examples of lions, tigers, and wolves to represent the word carnivore. The language clue (*such as*) is in italics.

H. Find the following words (printed in italics) in the reading passage. Write the definition clue and then the definition of the word.

Example: complex

language clue _ or _____

definition _ complicated _____

1. interdependence
   language clue _____

   definition _____

2. vulnerable
   language clue _____

   definition _____

3. pharmaceuticals
   language clue _____

   definition _____

4. commercial logging
   language clue _____

   definition _____

5. industrial projects
   language clue _____

   definition _____

6. commercial agriculture
   language clue _____

   definition _____

7. albedo
   language clue _____

   definition _____

I. Your instructor will give you a new handout with a complete article. Read the article carefully and then answer the following questions.

1. Name three products we receive from the rain forest.

2. Explain why it is important to protect the natives.

3. What is the rosy periwinkle and why is it important?

4. Using your knowledge of the hydrological cycle and the carbon and oxygen cycle, explain how deforestation will disrupt the climate.

5. What are the three main causes of deforestation?

References

The Earth's Renewable Resources: Tropical Forests. Nairobi: United Nations Environment Programmer, GEMS: Global Environment Monitoring System, 1990.

Hayes, Randy. *Fact Sheet on Tropical Rainforests.* Stanford: Earth Day, 1990.

Linden, Eugene, "The Death of Birth." *Time* January 2, 1989: 32–36.

Linden, Eugene, "Playing with Fire." *Time* September 18, 1989: 80–82.

Chapter 4

The Ocean Ecosystem

Draw a line from the name of the country to the ocean that borders it.

Malaysia	Pacific
Greenland	Atlantic
Brazil	Arctic
Antarctica	Indian
Japan	Antarctic

A Look Behind/A Look Ahead

In chapter 3, we learned about the forest ecosystem, which includes the temperate deciduous forest, the tropical rain forest, and the taiga. We also learned what a niche is in an ecosystem, as well as the causes, effects, and solutions related to deforestation.

In this chapter, we will study the ocean ecosystem. First we will look at the abiotic component of this ecosystem by studying the ocean floor. Then we will look at the biotic component by studying the ocean food chain. Finally we will apply our knowledge of this ecosystem to learn about species interaction and an environmental problem that threatens this ecosystem: oil spills.

To the Student

By the end of this chapter, you will be able to:

1. name and locate the five major oceans of the world.
2. understand the physical characteristics of the ocean floor.

3. describe a typical ocean food chain.
4. differentiate between, and give examples of, different species interactions.
5. describe the causes and effects of oil spills.

After completing this chapter, return to this page and assess your own achievement in reaching these objectives.

Vocabulary Development

Vocabulary Guessing Strategies: Word Morphology

When you are reading something in English, there may be some vocabulary words that you don't understand. Because it takes time to look these words up in a dictionary, it will help to learn some strategies for accurately guessing the meaning of these words. One way to do this is to look at the *morphology* of the word, or the parts of a word.

A word can consist of a prefix, a base, and a suffix. Not every word, however, will have a prefix and/or a suffix. A *prefix* is one or more syllables that can be added to the front of a word or base, while a *suffix* can be added to the end. Their function is to change the meaning of the word. Many prefixes and suffixes come from the Latin or Greek languages.

Look at the following word that we will learn about in this chapter.

SYMBIOSIS
prefix   base   suffix

The meaning of the prefix, base, and suffix are:

> *sym* = with, same, together
> *bio* = life
> *sis* = noun suffix

Therefore, we can guess that the word *symbiosis* is a noun which means "living together."

A. The following list contains some common prefixes, their meanings, and examples of a word using each prefix. There are some blank spaces in the example column. Fill in these blanks with a word you have learned in this text.

Prefix	Meaning	Example
a-	without, not	_____
ad-, as-	to, toward	advance
auto-	self	_____
cat-, cata-	down, against, very	_____
con-, com-, col-	together, with	_____
dia-	through, across, between	diameter
de-	down, off	_____
dis-	apart, not	disregard
e-, ex-	out from	emit
ecto-, exo-	outside, external	exoskeleton
in-, im-	in, into	immigrate
il-, im-, in-, ir-	not	impossible
inter-	between, among	_____
intra-	within	intraspecific
pre-	before	prehistoric
re-	back, again	_____
sym-	with, same, together	symbiosis
sub-	under, down	submarine

B. Underline the suffixes in the following words.

active	largest	biotic	deforestation	sustainable
terrestrial	diversity	reddish	environmental	development
closely	darkness	closer	indigenous	interdependence
ecologist	diversify	realize	differentiate	mutualism

Now place the suffixes that indicate if a word is a noun, verb, adjective, or adverb into their appropriate places in the following chart. An example of each suffix type has been done for you.

noun -ment	*verb* -ify
adjective -ible	*adverb* -ly

C. Finally, many of the base, or root, words also come from Latin and Greek.

Base	Meaning
bio	life
geo	land, earth
carni	meat or flesh
cide	kill
herbi	grass
vor/vore	eat/eating
omn	all
terr	land, earth
aqu(a)	water
chlor	green
phyll	leaf
photo	light
hydr	water
lith	stone
heter	different, other
troph	to nourish or grow

Using your lists of prefixes, suffixes, and bases, make a list of some of the words you have learned in this textbook and write their definitions.

1. _____

2. _____

3. _____

4. _____

5. _____

6. _____

7. _____

8. _____

9. _____

10. _____

D. Look at the vocabulary words from this chapter. Next to each word, write an *N* if you think the word is a noun, *V* if the word is a verb, *A* if the word is an adjective, and *AV* if the word is an adverb. Use any suffixes in the words to help you. Next, see if there are any prefixes or root words that can help you guess the meaning of the word. When you are finished with the chapter, return to this list to make sure you understand all of the words.

tributary (N)	comparative ( )	superlative ( )
continental margin ( )	continental shelf ( )	abyssal plain ( )
trench ( )	ocean ridge ( )	floor ( )
extend ( )	oceanographer ( )	resource ( )
sediment ( )	dump ( )	descended ( )
volcano ( )	earthquake ( )	elevation ( )
species interaction ( )	symbiosis ( )	predation ( )
mutualism ( )	commensalism ( )	competition ( )
intraspecific ( )	interspecific ( )	fossil fuel ( )
petroleum ( )	oil spill ( )	oil slick ( )
tanker ( )	buoyancy ( )	hull ( )
competitive exclusion ( )	phytoplankton ( )	zooplankton ( )
pelagic ( )	benthic ( )	baleen ( )

_____ _____ _____

I. The Oceans of the World

Oceans and seas cover 71% of the earth's surface. There are five major oceans: the Pacific, the Atlantic, the Indian, the Arctic, and the Antarctic. Each of these major oceans include smaller bodies of water that are connected to them. For example, the Baltic, Mediterranean, and Black Seas are each a part of the Atlantic Ocean.

A. Look at the following map and identify the five major oceans.

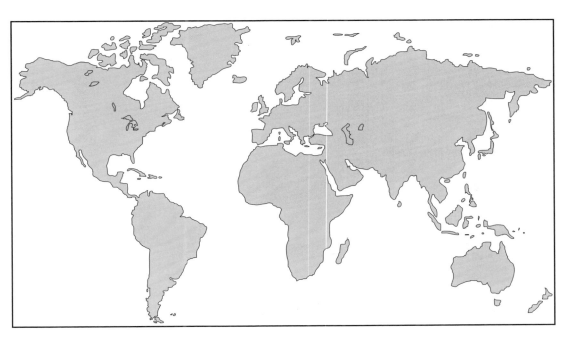

Oceans of the World

Body of Water	Area thousands of km²	thousands of mi²	Mean Depth meters	feet
Oceans				
Arctic	14,090	5,440	1,205	3,954
North Pacific	83,462	32,225	3,858	12,658
South Pacific	65,521	25,298	3,891	12,766
North Atlantic	46,744	18,059	3,285	10,778
South Atlantic	37,364	14,426	4,091	13,423
Indian	81,602	31,507	4,284	14,056
Antarctic (Southern)	32,249	12,451	3,730	12,238
Tributaries to the Arctic Ocean				
Norwegian Sea	1,383	534	1,742	5,716
Greenland Sea	1,205	465	1,444	4,738
Barents Sea	1,405	542	229	751
White Sea	90	35	89	292
Kara Sea	883	341	118	387
Laptev Sea	650	251	519	1,703
East Siberian Sea	901	348	58	190
Chukchi Sea	582	225	88	289
Beaufort Sea	476	184	1,004	3,294
Baffin Bay	689	266	861	2,825
Tributaries to the North and South Atlantic				
North Sea	600	232	91	299
Baltic Sea	386	149	86	282
Mediterranean Sea	2,516	971	1,494	4,902
Black Sea	461	178	1,166	3,826
Caribbean Sea	2,754	1,063	2,491	8;173
Gulf of Mexico	1,543	596	1,512	4,961
Gulf of Saint Lawrence	238	92	127	417
Hudson Bay	1,232	476	128	420
Gulf of Guinea	1,533	592	2,996	9,830
Tributaries to the Indian Ocean				
Red Sea	450	174	558	1,831
Persian Gulf	241	93	40	131
Arabian Sea	3,863	1,492	2,734	8,970
Bay of Bengal	2,172	839	2,586	8,485
Andaman Sea	602	232	1,096	3,596
Great Australian Bight	484	187	950	3,117
Tributaries to the North Pacific				
Gulf of California	177	68	818	2,684
Gulf of Alaska	1,327	512	2,431	7,976
Bering Sea	2,304	890	1,598	5,243
Sea of Okhotsk	1,590	614	859	2,818
Sea of Japan	978	378	1,752	5,748
Yellow Sea	417	161	40	131
East China Sea	752	290	349	1,145
Sulu Sea	420	162	1,139	3,737
Celebes Sea	472	182	3,291	10,798
Tributaries to Both the North and South Pacific				
South China Sea	3,685	1,423	1,060	3,478
Makassar Strait	194	75	967	3,173
Molukka Sea	307	119	1,880	6,168
Ceram Sea	187	72	1,209	3,967
Tributaries to the South Pacific				
Java Sea	433	167	46	151
Bali Sea	119	46	411	1,348
Flores Sea	121	47	1,829	6,001
Savu Sea	105	41	1,701	5,581
Banda Sea	695	268	3,064	10,053
Ceram Sea	187	72	1,209	3,967
Timor Sea	615	237	406	1,332
Coral Sea	4,791	1,850	2,394	7,855
Arafura Sea	1,037	400	197	646

B. Look at the table on page 74 describing the areas and depths of the oceans of the world. Quickly scan this chart to answer the following questions.

    1.   Of the five major oceans, which is the largest? the deepest?

    2.   Of the tributaries to the Indian Ocean, which has the greatest mean depth?

    3.   Which is bigger: the Bali Sea or the Flores Sea?

    4.   Which sea of all the tributaries has the greatest mean depth?

C. Underline the words in the questions from Activity B with the suffixes -er and -est. What part of speech is a word that has one of these suffixes?

Comparatives and Superlatives

When we want to compare two things using adjectives or adverbs in English, we use the comparative and superlative forms. For example, look at the following sentences.

The Indian Ocean is *deeper* than the Antarctic Ocean.
When we compare only two things, we use the *comparative* form.

The Indian Ocean is the *deepest* ocean of all the oceans in the world.
When we compare more than two things, we use the *superlative* form.

When forming the comparative or superlative form for one syllable adjectives or two syllable adjectives ending in *-y:*

a) comparatives are formed by adding an *-er* ending to the regular form
b) superlatives are formed by adding an *-est* ending

Regular	Comparative	Superlative
big	bigger	biggest
early	earlier	earliest

For longer adjectives and for adverbs that end with *-ly:*

a) form the comparative by adding the word *more* before the adjective or adverb
b) form the superlative by adding the word *most*

Regular	Comparative	Superlative
beautiful	more beautiful	most beautiful
carefully	more carefully	most carefully

Finally, a small group of fairly common adjectives and adverbs form their comparatives and superlatives in irregular ways.

Regular	Comparative	Superlative
good	better	best
bad	worse	worst
many	more	most
much	more	most
some	more	most
little	less or littler	least or littlest
well	better	best
badly	worse	worst

D. Using the table from page 74, write sentences about the oceans of the world using the comparative or superlative form.

1.

2.

3.

4.

5.

II. The Ocean Floor

The ocean floor can be classified into four major features: *continental margins, abyssal plains, trenches*, and *ocean ridges*.

A. Soon we are going to listen to a passage about the ocean floor, but, first, let's try to guess the meaning of some vocabulary words you will hear.

Vocabulary Guessing Strategies: Context

We already discussed one strategy—looking at the parts, or the morphology, of the word—for guessing a vocabulary word we don't know. Another strategy is to make a guess based on the surrounding context. For example:

The deer _____ when it saw the wolf.

In this sentence, we know that the missing word is a verb. We can also guess that the word is *ran*, because this is something we expect a deer to do when it sees a wolf. Let's look at another example.

Sharks can *zero in on* an injured fish from a quarter mile or more away.

You might read this sentence and not know the meaning of the phrasal verb *zero in on*. However, you can guess the meaning based on the phrase *from a quarter mile away* that it means something like *to see*.

We use this strategy of guessing from context often in our native languages. For some reason, however, we never feel very confident in our guessing abilities in a second language. Try reading a passage and then guess a few words. Check the dictionary to see if you are right. If you practice this strategy often, you will not only get better at guessing, but you should also become more confident in your abilities!

Read the following sentences and try to guess the meaning of the italicized word based on the context. Write your definition under the sentence. Then check your guess in a dictionary.

1. The continental shelf begins at the shore and *extends* seaward to a range of seventy to four hundred meters.

2. My brother loves studying about the ocean, so he became an *oceanographer.*

3. Oil and gas are important *natural resources* found in the rocks in the continental shelf.

4. The *sediment* at the bottom of the jar consisted mostly of mud and rocks.

5. Rivers *dump* their sediments in the ocean.

6. The airplane *descended* from 8,000 to 4,000 feet in elevation.

7. The liquid, red lava that comes from a *volcano* is very hot.

8. The *earthquake* shook the earth so hard that the apartment building collapsed.

9. The *abyss* at the bottom of the ocean is so deep you could fit a skyscraper into it!

B. Now listen to the passage, and fill in the diagram using these words.

continental margin   abyssal plain   ocean ridge
trench   continental rise   continental slope
continental shelf

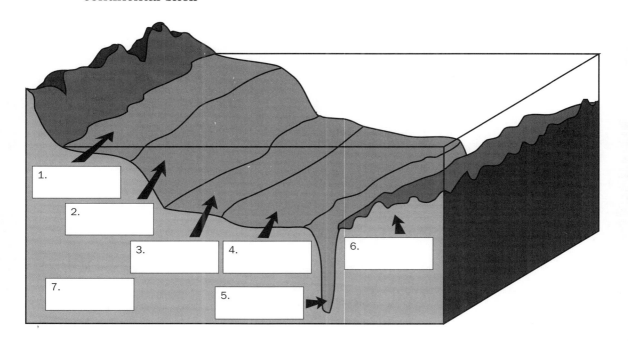

C. Finally, listen to the passage again and decide if the following statements are true (*T*) or false (*F*).

   1. The average elevation of the land is higher than the average
elevation of the ocean floor. ___

   2. Trenches in the ocean floor are found in places like Hawaii that
have earthquakes and volcanos. ___

   3. Abyssal plains are the deepest part of the ocean. ___

   4. The average depth of the continental shelf is 660 meters. ___

   5. The continental slope contains many natural resources. ___

III. Ocean Life and the Food Chain

A. Now listen to the lecture about life in the ocean and choose which
outline matches the lecture.

Ocean Life

I. Pelagic life

    A. Pelagic provinces

       1. Neritic province

          a.

          b.

       2. Oceanic province

          a.

          b.

    B. Pelagic forms

       1. Planktonic

       2. Nektonic

II. Benthic life

    A.

    B.

    C.

Ocean Life

I. Pelagic life

    A. Pelagic provinces

       1. Nektonic province

          a.

       2. Oceanic province

          a.

    B. Pelagic forms

       1. Planktonic

       2. Neritic

II. Benthic life

    A.

    B.

Organization by Classification

In the last chapter, we learned techniques for taking lecture notes, such as note-taking symbols and abbreviations to help you take notes faster, and recognizing language clues a speaker uses in introductions.

In the lecture you just heard about ocean life, the speaker uses several language clues for organization. The dominant organizational pattern the speaker uses is *classification*, which provides the listener with the main ideas and their subideas. Here are some language clues a speaker can use with this organizational pattern.

X can be
  classified into . . .
  broken down into . . .
  divided into . . .

There are 2 (3, 4, etc.)
  kinds of . . .
  groups of . . .
  types of . . .

The lecturer also uses certain language clues to provide definitions (*X is*, or *X means*), and also to compare and contrast the pelagic provinces and life in the pelagic zone (*likewise, similarly, however, on the other hand*, etc.—review the transitional expressions for comparison/contrast we learned about in chapter 3).

B. Now listen to the lecture again, focusing on the organizational clues for classification, definition, and comparison/contrast. Fill in as much of the correct outline in Activity A as you can.

C. Read the following passage about ocean food chains. Write the names of the animals (in italics) in their appropriate places in the food chains at the end of the passage. Two animals have been written in for you.

    Plankton are tiny, microscopic plants and animals that are at the lowest part of the food chain, and are therefore the most numerous. There are two types of plankton: phytoplankton and zooplankton. *Phytoplankton*, which are planktonic, or free-floating, are plants that live in the top part of the ocean because they need light for photosynthesis. *Zooplankton* are free-floating animals that feed on the phytoplankton. One type of zooplankton is called *krill*.

    Like every food chain, the amount of available energy decreases as you go up the food chain. Therefore, it takes ten thousand pounds of phytoplankton to make about a thousand pounds of krill, which in turn makes only a hundred pounds of *fish*, which makes ten pounds of *seal* to make one pound of *killer whale*.

Killer whales are called toothed whales; however, most of the whales found in the ocean are *baleen whales*, which are toothless but have rows of plates in their mouths (baleen) that strain the krill from the water. The largest baleen whale—the blue whale—may gather as much as three tons of krill a day by swimming along with its mouth open. Because the baleen whale feeds directly on krill, its food chain is much more efficient than the toothed whale food chains; it only takes a hundred pounds of phytoplankton to make a pound of baleen whale.

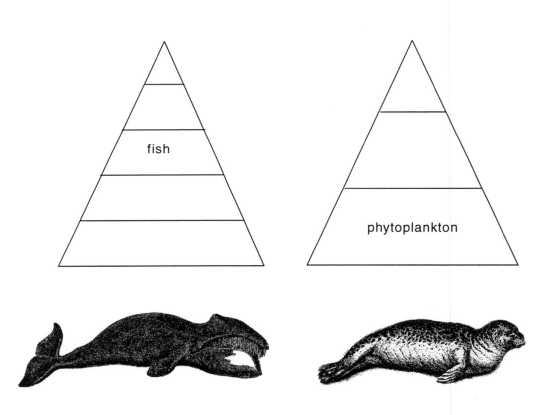

D. Of course, different types of food chains are found at the various levels of the ocean. This diagram shows some of the ocean plants and animals that inhabit different depths. Can you name a food chain that occurs at the top of the ocean? the bottom?

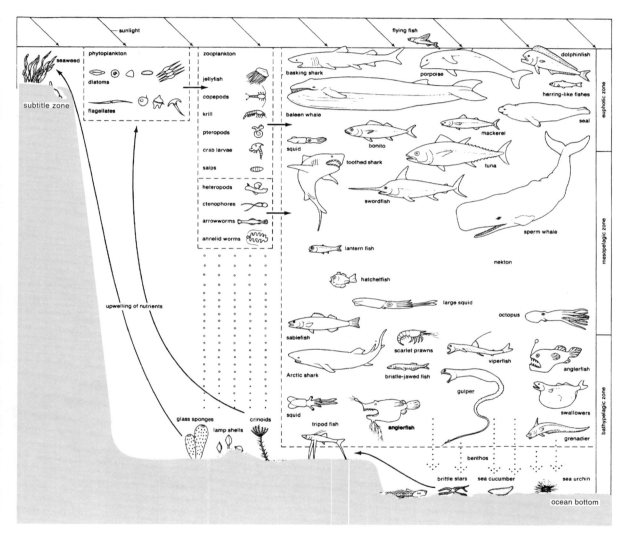

From *Encyclopedia Macropedia Encyclopedia*, vol. 14 (Chicago: Encyclopædia Britannica, 1993), 1167.

IV. Species Interaction

Organisms themselves play a large role in determining the structure of the ecosystem. For example, as we learned in chapter 3, the niche, or job, of an animal is part of this structure.

In this section, we will look at how living things in an ecosystem interact with each other in certain ways. There are three main types of these species interactions: *symbiosis, competition,* and *predation.*

A. *Symbiosis* is the relationship between two different species that live in close contact with each other. Look at the definitions for the three types of symbiosis. Following these definitions are several examples. Read each example and try to guess what type of symbiosis is being discussed. The first one has been done for you.

In *mutualism,* both species benefit from the association.
In *commensalism,* one species benefits from the association while the other is neither harmed nor helped.
In *parasitism,* one species benefits (the parasite), and the other species is harmed (the host).

Example: The clown fish brings food to the anemone and the anemone protects the clown fish from predators.

mutualism

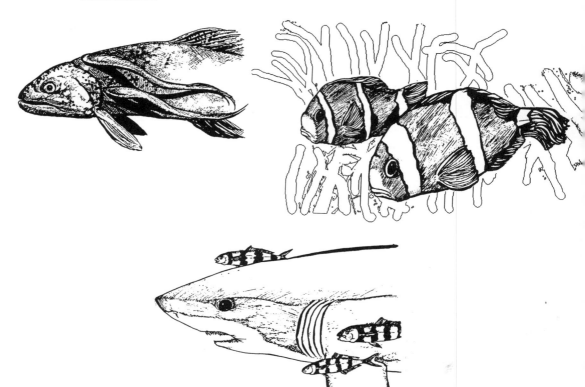

1. The remora attaches itself to the underside of a shark and gets free transportation, free protection, and free food by eating floating scraps from the shark's meal. In return, the remora gets rid of any parasites on the shark.

2. Lampreys, which look like snakes, attach themselves to salmon and drain the blood and body fluids from them. Lampreys are sometimes called the vampires of the sea.

3. The striped pilot fish swims alongside, under, and in front of the shark to catch any scraps of meat that the shark doesn't eat.

B. Quickly read the following passage about *competition.* Although many of the words have been deleted, see if you can answer the questions that follow.

Competition occurs when two or more species in the same ecosystem want to use the same _____ , such as light, temperature, nutrients, or anything that is especially important for survival in the ocean.

Two _____ of competition take place: intraspecific and interspecific. Intraspecific _____ is the interaction between two or more individuals of the _____ _____ species competing for something. For example, the interaction between killer whales, which feed on seals and therefore must compete for this food, is intraspecific _____ _____ . Interspecific _____ is the _____ between members of different species with _____ resource needs. Competition will therefore be _____ when resources are low and the population is high.

Research shows that no two species can occupy the exact niche in an _____ . If they do, one of the species will eventually die or become extinct, move, or adapt to use a different resource. This _____ is called the principle of competitive exclusion.

1. What are the two types of competition?

2. When is there the most competition among species?

3. What is the principle of competitive exclusion?

Vocabulary Guessing Strategies: Ignoring or Skipping Words

Although many of the words in the previous passage have been deleted, you can still understand the main ideas. Thus, there are many times that you can simply ignore vocabulary words that you don't understand, if you are only interested in understanding general ideas.

Before you reach for your dictionary, decide if you can simply ignore the word or can guess the word from its morphology or from the surrounding context. If you don't succeed with any of these strategies, and the word is important, then your dictionary is an appropriate tool to use.

C. To practice using the skills you have learned for guessing vocabulary through morphology and context, fill in each blank in the passage about competition with a word from the following choices. Some of the words can be used more than once.

similar	resources	ecosystem	highest	types
interaction	rule	same	extinct	species
competition				

D. *Predation*, the third type of species interaction, occurs when one organism (the predator) captures and feeds on an organism of another species (prey). Can you think of some predators in the ocean? What do you think their prey is?

E. Give an example using ocean organisms for each of the following relationships. Use the information you have learned in this chapter, or, if possible, visit a library.

mutualism:

commensalism:

parasitism:

competition:

predation:

V. Environmental Application: Oil Spills

A. Before we learn about an environmental problem that threatens the ocean ecosystem, brainstorm a list of at least five reasons why oceans are important.

B. Read the following passage.

OIL SPILLS

Oil is a natural product found in rocks inside the earth. It is called a fossil fuel, because it was created millions of years ago by the decomposition of plants and animals, and it can be burned to release energy. Oil is also called petroleum. This word comes from the two Latin words, *petra,* meaning *rock,* and *oleum,* meaning *oil.*

Although oil is very useful, it also is a contributor to ocean pollution. Over the past twenty-five years, crude oil has been accidentally spilled into the world's oceans hundreds of times. Oil spills result from two primary causes. The first cause is leakage from offshore oil wells. The second cause is tankers that carry oil and hit other ships, or hit the bottom of the ocean, breaking open the hull of the tanker. Oil spills form a widespread film of oil atop the water. This floating film is called an oil slick.

The slicks created by large spills have harmful direct and indirect effects. Animals that live on the surface of the water, such as birds and sea otters, suffer from direct effects. Sea otters rely on their fur to keep them warm and to help them float. Oil coats the fur, and it loses its ability to hold air bubbles, so the water reaches their skin and they die from freezing. Sea otters also ingest the oil when they clean their fur, and this too leads to death. Indirect effects of the oil spill occur when marine animals eat food or drink water that has been poisoned by the oil.

One example of a terrible oil spill occurred on March 24, 1989, when the oil tanker *Exxon Valdez* ran aground near Valdez, Alaska. More than 10 million gallons of crude oil spilled from the tanker's torn hull into Prince William Sound. As a result, at least 350,000 seabirds, 3,500 sea otters, and 136 bald eagles died. (Casey Bukro, "Greatest Oil Spill—How Terrible Was It?" *Chicago Tribune*, July 14, 1991)

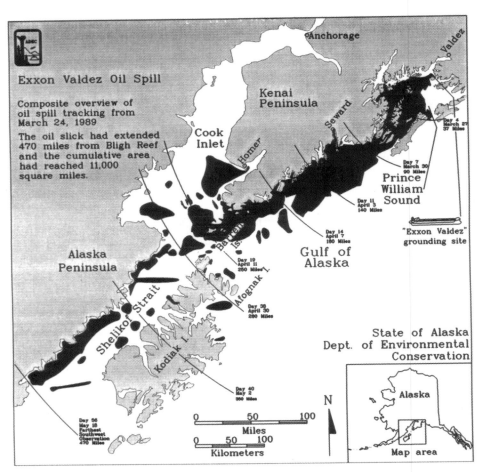

Exxon Valdez Oil Spill. (From the Alaska Department of Environmental Conservation.)

C. Sometimes readers make outlines of a passage in order to understand it better. Fill in the outline for this passage on oil spills, using the diagram on this page. Some of the diagram has been filled in for you.

Outlines

Outlines are visual tools that represent the relationship between, and importance of, ideas. Outlines are useful when listening to a lecture, or when taking notes on a reading. Look at the format of the blank outline diagram. When you write an outline, especially if your instructor asks you to turn one in, keep in mind some of these guidelines.

1. Place ideas of equal importance at corresponding levels. For example, all the main ideas in an outline should go under the roman numerals (I, II, III), the next important ideas should go under the capital letters (A,B,C), etc.
2. Move from the very general at the first level (roman numerals) to the more specific as you progress down the levels (capital letters, ordinal numbers, etc.). In other words, the items listed next to a capital letter or an ordinal number are the supporting details for the main idea listed next to the Roman numeral.

OUTLINE FOR READING ON OIL SPILLS

   I. Oil is a fossil fuel

  II.

      A.

      B.

 III.

      A.

         1.

         2. Ingest the oil—poisonous

B.

IV.

    A.   10 million gallons

    B.

D. Do the following experiment(s) about oil spills.

How Does an Ocean Oil Spill Affect Wildlife?

Materials
cooking oil or dirty motor oil
three hard-boiled eggs
bird feathers or, if not possible,
   cotton balls

shallow aluminum pan
magnifying glass

Procedure

Eggs:
1. Fill the aluminum pan with water. Add oil to the water to simulate an oil spill.
2. Add three hard-boiled eggs.
3. Remove one egg after five minutes. Peel off the shell and examine the egg. Remove and examine the second egg after 15 minutes, and the third egg after 30 minutes.
4. Write your observations.

Feathers:
1. Look at the feather under the magnifying glass.
2. Dip the feather into water for one minute and look at it again.
3. Dip the feather into oil for one minute and examine it with the magnifying glass.
4. Write your observations.

From Ovid K. Wong, *Hands on Ecology* (Children's Press: Chicago, 1991).

E. Based on the results of these experiments, write a short essay about the effect of oil spills on ocean birds.

Chapter 5

The Tundra Ecosystem

Circle any of the vocabulary words below that you think apply to the tundra. When you finish the chapter, return to this page and check to see if you were right!

hot	wind	snakes
productive	monkeys	snow
trees	snowshoe hares	willow
fragile	sand	cold
caribou	lichens	tigers

A Look Behind/A Look Ahead

In the last chapter we learned about the abiotic and biotic features of the ocean ecosystem, and we applied that knowledge to our study of oil spills. We also learned how species interact with one another through symbiosis, competition, and predation.

In this chapter we will study the tundra, which is a cold region where trees cannot grow. The tundra ecosystem covers approximately 9 million square miles in the Northern Hemisphere and is divided into two types: the arctic tundra, which is approximately 60% of the total tundra area, and the alpine tundra, which is approximately 40% of the total tundra area. The arctic tundra lies between the tree line and the Arctic Circle. The alpine tundra, which lies above the tree line and below the cap of snow on almost all of the earth's high mountains, is created by altitude rather than latitude. The plants and animals that live in these two types of tundra are very similar. There are minor differences, however, in the climate.

After learning about the living and nonliving things in the tundra, we will apply that knowledge of the tundra to a study about the impact of oil exploration in the Arctic National Wildlife Refuge in Alaska.

To the Student

At the completion of this chapter, you will be able to:

1. describe the physical characteristics of the tundra.
2. classify the plants and animals of the tundra.
3. understand the dynamics of a population.
4. describe and analyze the arguments for and against oil exploration in the Arctic National Wildlife Refuge.

After completing this chapter, return to this page and assess your own achievement in reaching these objectives.

Vocabulary Development

A good English-English dictionary can tell you much more about a word than just the meaning. Each dictionary will probably use slightly different abbreviations and formats; however, the following entries from *The American Heritage Dictionary of the English Language* should be consistent with most dictionaries. The specific format used by your dictionary will be explained in the front of the dictionary.

1.   2.   3.

[mi-grate (mī′grāt′)] *intr.v.* [-grated, -grating, -grates] 1. To move from one country or region and settle in another. 2. To change location periodically; move seasonally from one region to another: *"The birds that fish the cold sea for a living must either migrate or starve"* (Rachel Carson). [[Latin *migrāre.*] See mei-¹ in Appendix.*]   8.

5.

1.   2.   4.

[per-ma-nent (pûr′-mə-nənt)] *adj.* [*Abbr.* perm.]; 1. Fixed and
changeless; lasting or meant to last indefinitely. 2. Not expected
to change, in status, condition, or place: *permanent address; permanent secretary to the president—n.* 1. A permanent wave
(see). 2. A long-lasting hair setting. [Middle, from Old French,
from Latin *permanēs*, present participle of *permanēre,* to remain
throughout : *per-*, throughout + *manēre,* to remain [(see men-³ in
Appendix.*).]] —per′-ma-nent-ly *adv.*

8.

7.   6.

From *The American Heritage Dictionary of the English
Language,* 3d ed. (Boston: Houghton Mifflin Co., 1992).

A. Put the number from the dictionary entries on the line next to its
corresponding explanation.

___ Etymology (history of the word)
___ Part of speech (verb, noun, adjective, etc.)
___ Meaning(s) of the word
___ Spelling, syllabification, pronunciation
___ Cross references
___ Inflected forms (how the form of the word changes, usually by
changing the ending, to indicate different usages)
___ Undefined forms (forms of the main word [with the addition of
suffixes] that have the same meaning but different grammatical
functions)
___ Abbreviation

B. Now look at an entire page of entries from this same dictionary. Scan
it quickly for answers to the following questions.

1. How many syllables does the word *intendancy* have? What symbol does the dictionary use to separate the syllables?

2. Where is the stress in the word *intellect*? What symbol is used to
show where the stress is?

3. What part of speech is the word *intend*?

4. What other inflected forms are there of the word *intend*?

5. From what two languages did the word *intendant* come from?

integrating. **b.** The state of becoming integrated. **2.** The bringing of people of different racial or ethnic groups into unrestricted and equal association, as in society or an organization; desegregation. **3.** *Psychology.* The organization of the personality or social traits and tendencies of a personality into a harmonious whole. **4.** *Mathematics.* The process of finding the equation or function of which a given quantity or function is the derivative.

in·te·gra·tion·ist (ĭn′tĭ-grā′shə-nĭst) *n.* One who advocates or works for social integration. —**in′te·gra′tion·ist** *adj.*

in·te·gra·tor (ĭn′tĭ-grā′tər) *n.* **1.** One that integrates. **2.** An instrument for mechanically calculating definite integrals.

in·teg·ri·ty (ĭn-tĕg′rĭ-tē) *n.* **1.** Steadfast adherence to a strict moral or ethical code. See Synonyms at **honesty.** **2.** The state of being unimpaired; soundness. **3.** The quality or condition of being whole or undivided; completeness. [Middle English *integrite*, from Old French, from Latin *integritās*, soundness, from *integer*, whole, complete. See **tag-** in Appendix.]

in·teg·u·ment (ĭn-tĕg′yŏŏ-mənt) *n.* **1.** A natural outer covering or coat, such as the skin of an animal or the membrane enclosing an organ. **2.** *Botany.* The envelope of an ovule. [Latin *integumentum*, from *integere*, to cover : *in-*, on; see IN–[2] + *tegere*, to cover; see **(s)teg-** in Appendix.] —**in·teg′u·men′ta·ry** (-mĕn′tə-rē, -mĕn′trē) *adj.*

in·tel·lect (ĭn′tl-ĕkt′) *n.* **1.a.** The ability to learn and reason; the capacity for knowledge and understanding. **b.** The ability to think abstractly or profoundly. See Synonyms at **mind.** **2.** A person of great intellectual ability. [Middle English, from Old French *intellecte*, from Latin *intellēctus*, perception, from past participle of *intellegere*, to perceive. See INTELLECT.]

in·tel·lec·tion (ĭn′tl-ĕk′shən) *n.* **1.** The act or process of using the intellect; thinking or reasoning. **2.** A thought or an idea. [Middle English *intelleccioun*, understanding, from Latin *intellēctiō, intellēctiōn-*, synecdoche, from *intellēctus*, intellect. See INTELLECT.]

in·tel·lec·tive (ĭn′tl-ĕk′tĭv) *adj.* Of, relating to, or generated by the intellect. —**in′tel·lec′tive·ly** *adv.*

in·tel·lec·tron·ics (ĭn′tl-ĕk-trŏn′ĭks) *n. (used with a sing. verb).* The use of electronic devices to extend human intellect. [Blend of INTELLECT and ELECTRONICS.]

in·tel·lec·tu·al (ĭn′tl-ĕk′chōō-əl) *adj.* **1.a.** Of or relating to the intellect. **b.** Rational rather than emotional. **2.** Appealing to or engaging the intellect: *an intellectual book; an intellectual problem.* **3.a.** Having or showing intellect, especially to a high degree. See Synonyms at **intelligent.** **b.** Given to exercise of the intellect; inclined toward abstract thinking about aesthetic or philosophical subjects. —**intellectual** *n.* An intellectual person. [Middle English, from Old French *intellectuel*, from Late Latin *intellēctuālis*, from Latin *intellēctus*, intellect. See INTELLECT.] —**in′tel·lec′tu·al′i·ty** (-ăl′ĭ-tē) *n.* —**in′tel·lec′tu·al·ly** *adv.*

in·tel·lec·tu·al·ism (ĭn′tl-ĕk′chōō-ə-lĭz′əm) *n.* **1.** Exercise or application of the intellect. **2.** Devotion to exercise or development of the intellect. —**in′tel·lec′tu·al·ist** *n.* —**in′tel·lec′tu·al·is′tic** *adj.*

in·tel·lec·tu·al·i·za·tion (ĭn′tl-ĕk′chōō-ə-lĭ-zā′shən) *n. Psychology.* **1.** The act or process of intellectualizing. **2.** An unconscious means of protecting oneself from the emotional stress and anxiety associated with confronting painful personal fears or problems by excessive reasoning.

in·tel·lec·tu·al·ize (ĭn′tl-ĕk′chōō-ə-līz′) *tr.v.* **-ized, -iz·ing, -iz·es.** **1.** To furnish a rational structure or meaning for. **2.** To avoid psychological insight into (an emotional problem) by performing an intellectual analysis. —**in′tel·lec′tu·al·iz′er** *n.*

in·tel·li·gence (ĭn-tĕl′ə-jəns) *n. Abbr.* **int., I** **1.a.** The capacity to acquire and apply knowledge. **b.** The faculty of thought and reason. **c.** Superior powers of mind. See Synonyms at **mind.** **2.a.** *Theology.* An intelligent, incorporeal being, especially an angel. **b.** **Intelligence.** *Christian Science.* The primal, eternal quality of God. **3.** Information; news. See Synonyms at **news.** **4.a.** Secret information, especially about an actual or potential enemy. **b.** An agency or an office that gathers such information. **c.** Espionage agents, organizations, and activities considered as a group: *"Intelligence is nothing if not an institutionalized black market in perishable commodities"* (John le Carré).

intelligence quotient *n. Abbr.* **IQ, I.Q.** The ratio of tested mental age to chronological age, usually expressed as a quotient multiplied by 100.

in·tel·li·genc·er (ĭn-tĕl′ə-jən-sər, -jĕn′-) *n.* **1.** One who conveys news or information. **2.** A secret agent, an informer, or a spy.

intelligence test *n.* A standardized test used to establish an intelligence level rating by measuring a subject's ability to form concepts, solve problems, acquire information, reason, and perform other intellectual operations.

in·tel·li·gent (ĭn-tĕl′ə-jənt) *adj.* **1.** Having intelligence. **2.** Having a high degree of intelligence; mentally acute. **3.** Showing sound judgment and rationality: *an intelligent decision; an intelligent solution to the budget problem.* **4.** Appealing to the intellect; intellectual: *a film with witty and intelligent dialogue.* **5.** *Computer Science.* Having certain data storage and processing capabilities: *an intelligent terminal; intelligent peripherals.* [Latin *intellegēns, intellegent-*, present participle of *intellegere*, to perceive : *inter-*, inter- + *legere*, to choose; see **leg-** in Appendix.] —**in·tel′li·gen′tial** (-jĕn′shəl) *adj.* —**in·tel′li·gent·ly** *adv.*

SYNONYMS: *intelligent, bright, brilliant, knowing, quick-witted, smart, intellectual.* These adjectives mean having or showing mental keenness. *Intelligent* usually implies the ability to cope with demands arising from novel situations and new problems and to use the power of reasoning and inference effectively: *The most intelligent students do additional reading to supplement the material in the textbook. Bright* implies quickness or ease in learning: *Some children are brighter in one subject than in another. Brilliant* suggests unusually impressive mental acuteness: *"The dullard's envy of brilliant men is always assuaged by the suspicion that they will come to a bad end"* (Max Beerbohm). *Knowing* implies the possession of knowledge, information, or understanding: *Knowing furniture collectors bought American antiques before the prices soared. Quick-witted* suggests mental alertness and prompt response: *We were successful not because we were quick-witted but because we persevered. Smart* refers to quick intelligence and often a ready capability for taking care of one's own interests: *The smartest lawyers avoid the appearance of manipulating juries. Intellectual* stresses the working of the intellect and especially implies the capacity to grasp difficult or abstract concepts: *The scholar's interest in the intellectual and analytical aspect of music didn't prevent her from enjoying concerts.*

in·tel·li·gent·si·a (ĭn-tĕl′ə-jĕnt′sē-ə, -gĕnt′-) *n.* The intellectual elite of a society. [Russian *intelligentsiya*, from Latin *intelligentia*, intelligence, from *intelligēns, intelligent-*, intelligent. See INTELLIGENT.]

in·tel·li·gi·ble (ĭn-tĕl′ĭ-jə-bəl) *adj.* **1.** Capable of being understood: *an intelligible set of directions.* **2.** Capable of being apprehended by the intellect alone. [Middle English, from Old French *intelligibilis, intelligibilis*, from *intellegere*, to perceive. See INTELLIGENT.] —**in·tel′li·gi·bil′i·ty, in·tel′li·gi·ble·ness** *n.* —**in·tel′li·gi·bly** *adv.*

in·tem·per·ance (ĭn-tĕm′pər-əns, -prəns) *n.* **1.** Lack of temperance, as in the indulgence of an appetite or a passion. **2.** Excessive use of alcoholic beverages.

in·tem·per·ate (ĭn-tĕm′pər-ĭt, -prĭt) *adj.* Not temperate or moderate; excessive, especially in the use of alcoholic beverages. —**in·tem′per·ate·ly** *adv.* —**in·tem′per·ate·ness** *n.*

in·tend (ĭn-tĕnd′) *v.* **-tend·ed, -tend·ing, -tends.** —*tr.* **1.** To have in mind; plan: *We intend to go. They intend going. You intended that she go.* **2.a.** To design for a specific purpose. **b.** To have in mind for a particular use. **3.** To signify or mean. —*intr.* To have a design or purpose in mind. [Middle English *entenden*, from Old French *entendre*, from Latin *intendere* : *in-*, toward; see IN–[2] + *tendere*, to stretch; see **ten-** in Appendix.]

in·ten·dance (ĭn-tĕn′dəns) *n.* **1.** The function of an intendant; management. **2.** An administrative office or district.

in·ten·dan·cy (ĭn-tĕn′dən-sē) *n., pl.* **-cies.** **1.** The position or function of an intendant. **2.** Intendants considered as a group. **3.** The district supervised by an intendant, as in Latin America.

in·ten·dant (ĭn-tĕn′dənt) *n.* **1.** An administrative official serving a French, Spanish, or Portuguese monarch. **2.** A district administrator in some countries of Latin America. [French, from Old French, administrator, from Latin *intendēns, intendent-*, present participle of *intendere*, to intend. See INTEND.]

in·tend·ed (ĭn-tĕn′dĭd) *adj.* **1.** Deliberate; intentional: *"The only option is whether these will be purposeful, intended policies or whether they will be . . . concealed ones"* (Daniel Patrick Moynihan). **2.** Prospective; future: *an intended trip abroad next month.* —**intended** *n. Informal.* A person who is engaged to be married: *our daughter and her intended.* —**in·tend′ed·ly** *adv.*

in·tend·ing (ĭn-tĕn′dĭng) *adj.* Purposing to become or be; prospective: *intending lawyers; an intending contributor.*

in·tend·ment (ĭn-tĕnd′mənt) *n.* The true meaning or intention of something, especially of a law.

in·ten·er·ate (ĭn-tĕn′ə-rāt′) *tr.v.* **-at·ed, -at·ing, -ates.** To make tender; soften. [IN–[2] + Latin *tener*, tender; see TENDER[1] + –ATE[1].] —**in·ten′er·a′tion** *n.*

in·tense (ĭn-tĕns′) *adj.* **-tens·er, -tens·est.** **1.** Possessing or displaying a distinctive feature to an extreme degree: *the intense sun of the tropics.* **2.** Extreme in degree, strength, or size: *intense heat.* **3.** Involving or showing strain or extreme effort: *intense concentration.* **4.a.** Deeply felt; profound: *intense emotion.* **b.** Tending to feel deeply: *an intense writer.* [Middle English, from Old French *intens*, from Latin *intēnsus*, stretched, intent, from past participle of *intendere*, to stretch, intend. See INTEND.] —**in·tense′ly** *adv.* —**in·tense′ness** *n.*

SYNONYMS: *intense, fierce, vehement, violent.* The central meaning shared by these adjectives is "of an extreme kind": *intense emotions; fierce loyalty; vehement dislike; violent rage.*
USAGE NOTE: The meanings of *intense* and *intensive* overlap considerably, but the two are often subtly distinct. When used to describe human feeling or activity, *intense* often suggests a strength or concentration that arises from inner dispositions and is particularly appropriate when used to describe emotional states: *intense pleasure, dislike, loyalty,* and so forth. *Intensive* is more frequently applied when the strength or concentration of an activity is imposed from without: *intensive bombing, training, marketing.* Thus a reference to *Mark's intense study of German* suggests that Mark himself was responsible for the concentrated activity, whereas *Mark's intensive study of German* suggests that

6. This dictionary also gives labels for the level of the style of usage (nonstandard, informal, slang, vulgar, obsolete, archaic, rare, poetic, regional, British, foreign language). Find an example of one of these labels and write the word and the example below.

7. What are the undefined forms for the word *intense*?

8. For certain words, many dictionaries also provide synonyms (different words that have a similar meaning). What are two synonyms for the word *intelligent*?

C. Use your dictionary to look up any words you don't understand in this chapter. Keep a list of these words and study them often.

I. The Physical Characteristics of the Tundra

A. Listen to the following story about hiking in the alpine tundra. The speaker will discuss some important physical features. The first time that you listen, try to write down all the physical factors (one of them has been done for you). The second time you hear the passage, focus on writing down as many details about those factors as you can.

Physical Factor	Details
sunshine	

B. Imagine you are preparing for a backpacking trip to the alpine tundra. It is June, and you will camp for four nights. You have a long, uphill hike to your campsite (10 km), so you don't want your backpack to be too heavy. Therefore, you must think about what you will definitely take, what you would probably take, what you might take, or what you definitely won't take.

Modals

Modals (*can, could, may, might, shall, should, will, would,* and *must*) are types of verbs called helping verbs, or auxiliary verbs. Although modals can express many different things, they are often used to make predictions that can range from possibilities to certainties.

Possibility

may	I *may* take my camera on my trip.
might	I *might* take my camera on my trip.
could	I *could* take my camera on my trip.

Probability

would	I *would* take my camera on my trip.

Certainty

must	I *must* take my camera on my trip.
will	I *will* take my camera on my trip.
will not	I *won't* take my camera on my trip.

Look at the list of possible items you could take on your trip. If you think of anything else to take, add it to your list. Then, group the items according to what you will definitely take, what you probably would take, what you might take, or what you definitely won't take. Base your opinions on your knowledge of the physical characteristics of the alpine tundra. Here are some expressions that might help you.*

---

*Adapted from Leo Jones and Victoria Kimbrough, *Great Ideas.* (Cambridge: Cambridge University Press, 1987).

I don't think we'll need. . . .   I'd definitely like to take . . . .

Why would you need a . . . ?   I'd take. . . .

Another thing we'll need is . . . .   What/how about a . . . ?

A . . . wouldn't help/be useful.   Maybe a . . . would be helpful/ useful.

List of Items

suntan lotion	fishing pole	folding chair
extra socks	long underwear	extra shoes
coffee	toilet paper	sunglasses
camp stove	first aid kit	dried food
sleeping bag	cot	tent
pillow	hat	lantern
matches	mittens	map
bottle of liquor	flashlight	book
winter jacket	extra pants	bottle of water
canned food	shower kit	towel
aspirin	cooler	cooking equipment
camera	gun	windbreaker
compass	water purification tablets	

What will/would/might/won't you take?

II. Life in the Tundra

A. Unscramble the following words to make sentences that describe life in the tundra.

Example: short/chains/are/the/example/food/for/,

    For example, the food chains are short.

1. result/season/a/short/they/in/growing

2. ecosystem/the/is/it/simple/is/because/fragile

3. tundra/factors/alpine/of/because/limiting/also/is/fragile/the

4. very/life/the/alpine/is/fragile/in/tundra

5. change/significant/a/food/small/therefore/on/chain/has/any/effect/the/,

6. cold/are/limiting/shortage/these/factors/sun/of/and/a

B. Now make a coherent paragraph by putting the sentences from Activity A in order. First find the topic sentence and then use the tools of coherence (repetition of key words and logical connectors) that you learned about in chapter 2. When writing your paragraph, include the example sentence. The concluding sentence is provided.

As a result of the simplicity and short growing seasons, it takes a long time for the alpine tundra to recover from any damage.

C. Read the following passage that classifies plant and animal life in the tundra. Using your knowledge of the language that signals classification (see chapter 4), fill in the diagram on page 100 with the information in this text.

More than 99 percent of the plants in the tundra are perennials, or plants that grow more than two years. Annuals cannot grow in the tundra because of the short growing season.

Tundra plants can be classified into five main groups. Lichens are primitive plants without stems, leaves, or roots. They are a combination of algae and fungi that grow on rocks and the ground. A second group of plants are the mosses, which are usually found in cracks in rocks. Arctic cotton grass is a kind of grass, the third group of alpine plants, which produces a ball of white fluff that helps the plant stay warm. The tundra's most delicate-looking plants—the small flowering plants—are often the toughest. For example, the Arctic poppy has thin petals that remain on the flower even when it is extremely windy. Finally, a typical shrub in the alpine tundra is the ground willow.

Birds in the tundra are either migratory or permanent. The snowy owl, the ptarmigan, and the raven are birds that live in the tundra all year long. They have learned to survive the cold and the darkness of the winter. Two of these birds, the snowy owl and the ptarmigan, turn white in the winter. They change color so that they match the snowy background, which will help protect them from predators. With the coming of spring, however, other birds migrate to the tundra. Some of these typical migratory birds include geese, ducks, and terns.

Mammals are also both migratory and permanent residents of the tundra. The permanent residents can be further classified into three types: mammals that roam the open tundra year-round, mammals that hibernate, or mammals that dig tunnels under the snow. A typical migratory animal is the caribou, which migrates from the taiga in the spring. The chief predator of the caribou is the wolf, and this animal roams the open tundra year-round. Two other animals that roam the open tundra year-round are the Arctic hare—or snowshoe hare—and the Arctic fox. The hare and the fox turn white in the winter, just like the snowy owl and the ptarmigan, to protect themselves from predators or to surprise their prey. Grizzly bears and ground squirrels are animals that hibernate, but bears will sometimes come out of their dens during the winter. Finally, lemmings, which are small furry herbivores that look like hamsters, dig tunnels under the snow and live their lives much as they do above the ground in the summer.

Tundra Life

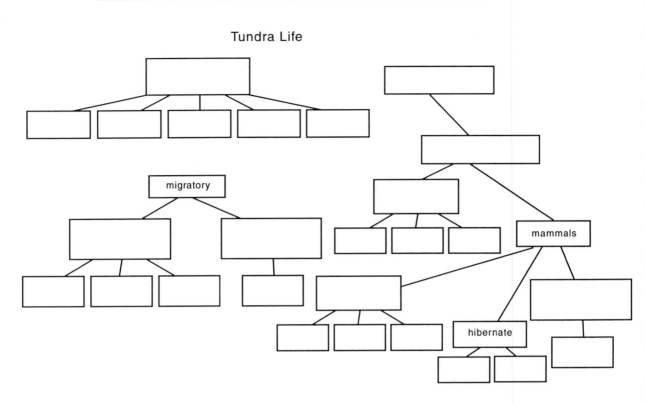

III. Population Dynamics

A. Read the passage and answer the questions that follow.

A population is a group of organisms belonging to one species that lives in the same geographic area. We can classify a population according to its *size* (the total number of members in the population) or the population *density* (the number of individuals per unit of space). For example, if there were one hundred mice in an area of ten square kilometers, the population density would be ten mice per square kilometer.

Populations are dynamic; in other words, their numbers go up and down over time. Yet, when we look at populations over a long period of time, their numbers remain relatively stable. Why?

The term *carrying capacity* refers to the maximum population that a certain area can support. Although all animals will reproduce beyond the actual carrying capacity of their environment (their *biotic potential*), *limiting factors* control the population so it stays at an appropriate level. These limiting factors can be divided into two categories: *density-dependent factors*, and *density-independent factors*. Density-dependent factors are biotic, and their effects are greater when the population density is high. These factors include predator/prey relationships, competition, stress, and disease. Density-independent factors, which are abiotic, include weather, food, water, and nutrients. Both density-dependent and density-independent factors help regulate the population; however, some factors will be more important than others for certain populations.

1. What is the main idea of this passage?
    a. Density-dependent and density-independent factors are different.
    b. A population goes up and down in size, but certain things keep it about the same.
    c. The size of a population is different than its density and has limiting factors.
2. Two populations can have the same size but have different densities.
    True   False
3. Which of the following would *not* be a density-dependent factor?
    a. lower reproductive rates due to crowding
    b. a drought due to a very hot summer
    c. the spread of an infectious disease in deer
4. Look at the following diagram. Which part of the diagram indicates biotic potential, limiting factors, and carrying capacity?

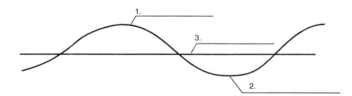

F. Look at the following graph showing the population cycles of the Canada lynx and the snowshoe hare. Decide if the statements about the graph are true or false by writing *T* or *F* next to each sentence.

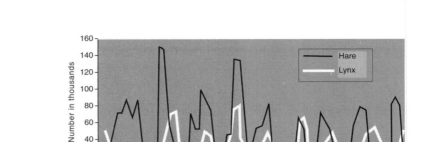

Reproduced from Thomas C. Emmel, *An Introduction to Ecology and Population Biology* (New York: W.W. Norton, 1973).

___ 1. The number of Canada lynx and snowshoe hares rises for several years, then drops sharply, again and again over a period of time.

___ 2. The size of the populations remains the same during a ten-year period.

___ 3. Even though the population numbers go up and down, their average size remains about the same over time.

___ 4. When the lynx population is high, the hare population decreases.

___ 5. When the lynx population is low, the hare population decreases.

Now answer these questions.

6. What is the carrying capacity of the lynx population? the hare population?

7. Why does the lynx population go up and down? (Hint: think about the relationship between the lynx and the hare.) Do density-dependent factors or density-independent factors control the lynx population?

C. Write about the population dynamics of the ecosystem where you live. The ecosystem could be your house, your neighborhood, or your city. What is the population size? What is the carrying capacity? What limiting factors control the population?

IV. Environmental Application: Oil Exploration in the Arctic National Wildlife Refuge

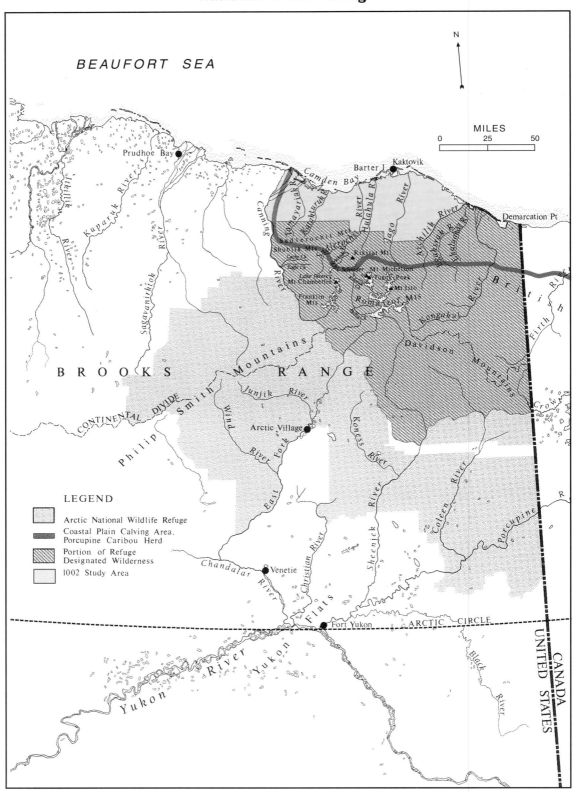

This map was designed and produced by Allison Frey, Wilma Frey Associates, Washington, D.C.

A. The following headings consist of the main ideas in the reading passage, "Oil and Wilderness." Skim the passage and write the appropriate heading on the line above each paragraph. The first has been done for you.

Oil Possibilities in the 1002 Area
What Is the Arctic National Wildlife Refuge (ANWR)
Congressional Action on the ANWR
History of the ANWR
Wildlife and People in the 1002 Area
Definition of the Problem

B. Read the passage.

OIL AND WILDERNESS

What Is the Arctic National Wildlife Refuge (ANWR)?

The Arctic National Wildlife Refuge (ANWR) is an area rich in fauna, flora, and oil potential. The land borders the Beaufort Sea at the northern tip of Alaska. In the summer, the snow melts, wildflowers rise in the plains, and great numbers of caribou arrive to give birth to their young. In September, the tundra freezes again, the sea hardens, grizzly bears hibernate, and daylight gets shorter.

The ANWR is the second largest, and northernmost, of the 437 units in the more than 90 million acres of the National Wildlife Refuge System in the United States. Sixteen of those units and 77 million of those acres lie in Alaska; 19,049,236 of those 77 million acres belong to the ANWR.

The coastal plain of the ANWR is currently the most promising U.S. onshore oil and gas prospect. On the other hand, the refuge is home to a spectacular variety of plants and animals. The presence of caribou, polar bears, grizzly bears, wolves, quantities of migratory birds, and many other species in a nearly undisturbed state have led some to call the area "America's Serengeti." The conflict between oil potential and nature creates a dilemma: should Congress open the area for oil and gas development, or should the area's unique ecosystem be given permanent protection?

The ANWR of today was established through the passage of the Alaska National Interest Lands Conservation Act (known as the

ANILCA or the Alaska Lands Act). Section 1003 of this act prohibited oil and gas development in the refuge unless authorized by Congress. However, Section 1002 of the law set aside 1.5 million acres in a 100-mile stretch of the coastal plain for study. This study was to evaluate the area's potential for oil and gas development and to weigh that potential against the impact of development on the land and its wildlife.

Estimates of economically recoverable petroleum reserves from the 1002 area range from less than 1 billion barrels to more than 9 billion barrels. The mean estimate is about 3.57 billion barrels. The chance of finding recoverable oil is 19%. Daily consumption in the U.S. is now approximately 18 million barrels, so even if the optimum figure of 9 billion barrels is recovered, it will only satisfy domestic consumption needs for at most about a year and a half (500 days).

Wildlife abounds in the ANWR. The 1002 area is an important piece of land because many animals migrate to this coastal plain for breeding and other activities. Tundra swans, shorebirds, and as many as 325,000 lesser snow geese migrate to fatten themselves on tundra vegetation. The Porcupine caribou herd, a group of approximately 170,000 animals, migrates annually to the 1002 area to feed on vegetation, birth and raise their calves, and escape the numerous insects. Some polar bears rely on the area to build their dens, and bowhead whales migrate past the area in September.

The Inupiat Eskimos of the village of Kaktovik live along the coast adjacent to the 1002 area. Kaktovik natives support leasing generally, but oppose leasing in the primary calving area, and want restrictions on discharging firearms. Two other native groups, the Athabascan Indians in Alaska (called Gwich'in Indians) and Canada, are subsistence hunters; caribou are their primary source of food. Therefore, they oppose leasing and support wilderness designation for the area.

The question of whether the ANWR will be opened to oil development will be decided by the United States Congress. Three choices exist for legislation.

1. Designate the area as protected wilderness, which would prevent energy development.
2. Pass legislation permitting energy leasing in the 1002 area.
3. Take no action. Because the current law prohibits development unless Congress acts, this option prevents energy development and allows more time to study the situation.

Option 3 is the one that has been chosen for the last several years by Congress.

C. Answer the following questions about the passage.

1. What are the three native groups involved in this debate. How do they feel about oil exploration in the ANWR?

2. What types of wildlife can be found in the ANWR? Why is the 1002 area especially important for some of these animals?

3. How big is the ANWR?

4. What is the 1002 area?

5. How much oil is predicted to be recoverable in the 1002 area? How long will that amount meet consumption needs in the United States?

6. What are the three legislative options for the ANWR?

D. The arguments for oil exploration are summarized in the following chart. After the chart, there is a list of counterarguments, or arguments against exploration. Match these counterarguments to the given arguments in their appropriate places in the chart. An example is provided.

Arguments for Exploration	*Arguments against Exploration*
Recovering these oil reserves would reduce dependence on foreign oil and insulate our energy markets from the recurring crises in the Middle East.	Even if the highest estimate of 9 billion barrels is recovered, it would take 10–15 years for oil to appear in any quantity. By then, security and market conditions are likely to be much different. Alternative energy sources could be developed in that same time.
Reducing dependence on foreign oil would promote a favorable balance of international trade. Replacing 600,000 barrels of imports per day at $16.80/barrel (May 1993 price) would reduce the trade deficit by 3.7 billion per year.	
Opening the area to development would provide federal, state, and local revenues.	

(*continued*)

Oil exploration would directly impact only a tiny percentage of the massive wildlife refuge. And millions of Americans would burn that oil compared to the handful of wilderness buffs who will ever view wolves and caribou in the most expensive tourist destination in the United States.	
Predicted impacts on most wildlife resources from exploration and development drilling are minor or negligible. Potential major effects on wildlife reproduction are limited to the Porcupine caribou herd and reintroduced musk oxen.	
Oil is the largest source of revenue for the state of Alaska; every Alaskan over 6 months of age receives a yearly tax-free dividend from the state for oil-related activities ($900.00 in 1989). Oil exploration creates jobs and comfortable living conditions. A billion dollars in tax revenue from oil in the last ten years has changed the daily lives of the residents of the Arctic; oil revenue has financed new oil-heated houses, gravel roads, electricity, and services such as schools, clinics, and satellite TV. Wages at construction sites average $26.00/hour.	

The Counterarguments: Arguments against Exploration

1. Caribou are the chief source of food for Alaskan and Canadian Athabascan Indian groups. These herds will be displaced from their calving grounds and disrupted by abnormal migration routes; if

forced to go inland, insects would bother them so much that they wouldn't eat enough food for their return migration. The coastal area is also crucial for vital stages in the life cycles of whales, birds, polar bears, and musk oxen.

2. If the market price of oil is low, it could take more money to produce the oil than would be realized by selling it. Also, much money is needed for the prevention and possible cleanup of disasters like oil spills or hazardous waste spills.

3. This "tiny percentage of the refuge" represents the least disturbed Arctic coastal area under U.S. ownership. Of the 1200 miles of Alaska's Arctic coastline, only the 105 miles in the 1002 area are protected. If the entire 1002 area were leased, the development would lead to approximately 5000 acres of vegetation being covered by gravel for roads, pipelines, airstrips, and other facilities. Physical disturbances such as erosion, dust, and pollution would alter the habitat value of many more acres. The possibility also exists for severe environmental damage through oil spills and the dangers of hazardous waste disposal.

4. If only 1 billion barrels were found, the favorable impact on the trade deficit would last less than a year (166 days).

5. The chances of finding recoverable oil reserves are only 19%. What happens if there isn't any oil? What happens when the oil runs out for good, and Alaska has no other industries with which to support itself?

E. Review the three options Congress has concerning the ANWR. Using your summary of the arguments for and against oil exploration, decide in groups which legislative choice you support, and why.

F. Look at the following sample letters about the ANWR. Who do you think these letters are intended for? What do you think the writer's purpose is for each of the samples?

Sample A

Dear Anwar:

Hi. How are you? Things are great here in Michigan, but it's a little cold. My classes are good. One is about Ecology, and I've learned so many things I didn't know. Right now we're studying about the Arctic National Wildlife Refuge. This is a place in Alaska that the government designated for wilderness. It seems like an awesome place, with polar bears, caribou, moose, wolves and tons of birds. We should visit there!! There's a problem though, cuz one area (called the 1002 area) is not protected and the US Congress is deciding if they should look for oil in the area.

It doesn't sound like there's that much oil—enough to last the US for only about a year. It doesn't seem worth it, does it? But many people think it will make the US more secure and less dependent on foreign oil. What do you think?

I hope things are great for you back home. Say hi to everyone.

Mohammed

Sample B
The Honorable Senator Smith
United States Senate
Washington, D.C. 20510

Dear Senator Smith:

As an Inupiat Indian living in Kaktovik, I encourage you
to vote for legislation permitting energy leasing in the
1002 area of the ANWR.

As you know, the ANCSA gave Alaskan natives land that is
included in the ANWR. However, the land we own is subject
to the laws and regulations that govern the refuge, so we
are unable to develop this land. Should energy development occur, our people would make money through either
the sale of the land or the discovery of oil. In addition,
many jobs would be created that would help both the economic and social situations in our village.

Our lifestyle has changed dramatically since the discovery of oil at Prudhoe Bay. Now that the oil is beginning to
dwindle at that development, it is even more important to
develop the ANWR land. We cannot go back to our old way of
life, and, other than oil, there are no real possibilities for making money in this area.

I appreciate your time, and know you will do what is best
for my people.

Sincerely,

A Kaktovik Native

Audience and Purpose

When you write something, it is important to consider your *audience*, that is, the people who will read what you have written, and your *purpose*, the reason for writing.

Knowing your audience will help you reach your goal of communicating clearly and effectively. Your audience will determine what you say and how you say it. You must consider what your audience knows and doesn't know. Your relationship with the reader will determine your content, your organization, your sentence structure, and your word choices.

You also must think about your purpose for writing. What do you want the reader to do with the information when they are finished reading? Some of the common purposes for writing are to entertain, to inform, to define, to describe, to persuade, to explain, or to express feelings.

G. How are Sample A and Sample B different? Make specific comments on the differences in content, organization, grammar, and word choice.

H. Write a letter to a U.S. Congressperson persuading them to support one of the three legislative options available to Congress concerning the ANWR. Write from the perspective of one of the following people.

1. yourself
2. an Athabascan Indian
3. a wildlife photographer for National Geographic
4. the president of an oil company
5. other: _____

Consider the current world oil prices, the stability of the Middle East, and the current economy of Alaska, along with other relevant issues.

References

Baldwin, Pam, and Lynne M. Corne. "The Arctic National Wildlife Refuge" *Congressional Research Service Report for Congress.* Washington, D.C.: The Library of Congress, 1993.

Drew, Lisa. "Here's Your Land, Now Make Money." *National Wildlife,* December–January 1992: 38–45.

Egan, Timothy. "The Great Alaska Debate: Can Oil and Wilderness Mix?" *New York Times Magazine,* August 4, 1991: 21–36.

Lee, Douglas. "Oil in the Wilderness. An Arctic Dilemma." *National Geographic,* Dec. 1988: 858–71.

Rogers, Michael. "In Alaska, the Future Is Now." *Newsweek,* September 18, 1989: 63–64.

Watkins, T. H. *Vanishing Arctic.* New York: Aperture Foundation, 1988.

Chapter 6

The Grassland Ecosystem

Find the names of some of the animals of the grassland ecosystem in the puzzle. You'll have to look from side to side, up and down, and diagonally.

f	l	p	o	c	k	e	t	g	o	p	h	e	r
o	j	w	o	n	x	d	b	e	h	l	r	a	g
c	a	b	o	t	m	n	w	o	l	f	n	e	c
l	c	f	b	l	q	s	l	p	z	t	o	f	o
d	k	w	i	l	f	e	b	e	e	s	i	u	y
y	r	f	s	s	o	b	m	l	b	c	l	y	o
m	a	e	o	r	p	r	o	w	r	i	d	h	t
k	b	q	n	f	b	p	p	f	a	n	o	v	e
x	b	x	c	h	e	e	t	a	h	h	t	n	g
e	i	w	p	k	a	n	g	a	r	o	o	a	q
d	t	c	s	a	t	u	v	j	m	l	b	w	h

lion

zebra

pocket gopher

bison

antelope

coyote

cheetah

jackrabbit

kangaroo

115

A Look Behind/A Look Ahead

In chapter 5, we studied the abiotic and biotic features of the tundra ecosystem. We learned about the dynamics of a population and about some of the factors that regulate a population. Finally, we applied our knowledge of the tundra ecosystem to analyze one environmental threat: oil exploration in the Arctic National Wildlife Refuge.

In this chapter we will look at the grassland ecosystem, and further study the idea that *ecosystems are dynamic.* They are constantly changing, yet they show a certain stability—the ability to tolerate or resist changes by outside influences, or to restore themselves after a disturbance like a fire. Finally, we will learn about the causes, effects, and possible solutions to global warming and desertification.

To the Student

After completing this chapter, you will be able to:

1. differentiate and describe the biotic and abiotic features of the tropical and temperate grassland ecosystems.
2. understand how ecosystems regulate themselves through the process of succession.
3. describe the causes and effects of global warming and evaluate various solutions to this problem.
4. define desertification and summarize the causes of, and possible solutions to, this problem.

After completing this chapter, return to this page and assess your own achievement in reaching these objectives.

Vocabulary Development

In chapter 4, we learned about suffixes, which can indicate the different parts of speech, like nouns, verbs, adjectives, and adverbs. In the dictionary, these forms are often listed as undefined forms at the end of a definition.

The following chart lists some of the vocabulary words you will encounter in this chapter. Complete the chart, keeping in mind that word formation may not be the same for all of the words, and that some boxes may remain empty.

Noun	Verb	Adjective	Adverb
	disturb		
		domestic	
ecology			
			successively
	establish		
prediction			
		accumulative	
			gradually
	colonize		

Use the following space to write any other new vocabulary words you find in this chapter. Include the word's definition.

I. The Physical Characteristics of the Grassland

A. We are going to listen to a short lecture about the physical characteristics of the grassland. What do you predict the lecture will discuss?

The lecture tells us two ways the grassland ecosystem is used by humans. What do you think these ways are?

Listen to the lecture one time to see if your predictions were correct.

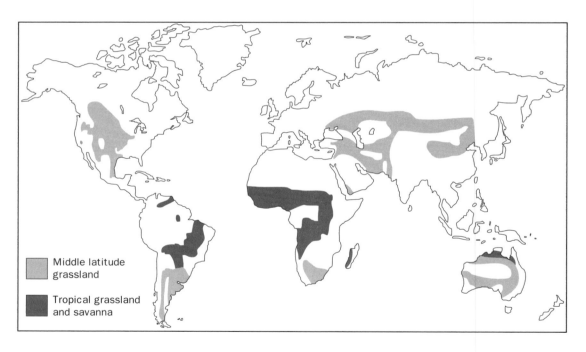

Grasslands of the World

B. Now listen to the lecture again. On a separate sheet of paper, take notes using note-taking symbols and abbreviations. Visually represent the information, using the following guidelines.

Taking Lecture Notes—Visually Representing Relationships in Note Taking

When taking notes on a talk, it will help if you show relationships between information items, including the relative importance of that information. There are several ways to do this.

Example: The grassland ecosystem develops where rainfall is high enough to keep deserts from forming, but low enough to prevent forests from growing. This type of ecosystem is found all over the world and can be divided into temperate or tropical grasslands. Temperate grasslands are found in Canada and the United States, Argentina, South Africa, Russia, and Australia.

defn: Grslnd – rnfl ↑ so no deserts; ↓ so no forests

Temperate   Tropical

U.S., Canada, S. Africa, Russia, Australia, Argentina

Notice how the arrangement of the notes shows how information relates to particular topics, as well as the relative importance of that information. Another way to arrange this information is to indent. More specific information is written under the general information and indented to the right.

defn: Grslnd – rnfl ↑ so no deserts; ↓ so no forests
   Temperate
       U.S., Canada, S. Africa, Russia, Argentina, Australia
   Tropical

Of course, there are other ways to visually represent the relationships and the relative importance of ideas. Whatever method you choose, make sure you are consistent, are using as few words as possible, and are accurately reflecting the relationships.

C. Answer the following questions using your lecture notes.

1. What is the average annual rainfall in the temperate grasslands?

2. Which grasslands are used primarily for agriculture?

3. Savannas are located in Russia—true or false?

4. Savannas get more rainfall than temperate grasslands—true or false?

5. Describe the climate in the temperate grasslands.

II. Life in the Grassland

A. Read the following passage about life in the grassland.

At one time the grassland occupied between 40 and 45 percent of the Earth's surface. Since the early 1800s, however, many of the natural plants and animals of the grassland have been eliminated by humans through hunting, nomadic and commercial grazing, and agriculture.

Because the climate and soil of the temperate grassland ecosystem is suitable for growing crops, most of this type of grassland has been converted to agricultural use. Before this conversion, the North American grassland was home to large herbivores, such as bison, pronghorn antelope, and elk. Wolves, coyotes, and Plains Indians preyed on these grazing animals.

Although most of these animals are gone, grasslands that haven't been disturbed contain numerous species of small herbivores, such as the ground squirrel, pocket gopher, and jackrabbit. These animals are preyed upon by snakes, weasels, badgers, and golden eagles. Herbivores such as the ground squirrel play important roles in mixing and providing oxygen for the soil. Prairie dogs, once the most numerous species of herbivore in the temperate grassland, have been eliminated by ranchers who thought they competed with the cattle for food.

The savanna, on the other hand, is not suitable for agriculture, but nomadic herding and commercial grazing of sheep, goats, and cattle over the past two hundred years has destroyed much of its natural condition. Recently, however, many game reserves have been established to protect the plants and animals. In these reserves in Africa there are large herds of grazing, hoofed mammals, such as the wildebeest, zebra, and antelope. These animals are preyed upon by large carnivores such as the lion and cheetah. Australian savannas are populated by species of the herbivorous kangaroo and wallaby, which are preyed upon by dingos. The ability of the kangaroo (and the jackrabbit in North America) to leap allows them to see above the tall grass to catch sight of predators.

B. Make food chains for both the temperate and tropical grasslands.

C. Look at the sentences below about the grassland. How do the sentences differ grammatically.

Indians have lived on the grassland for many years.
Indians lived on the grassland for many years.

Is there any difference in the meaning? If so, what?

D. Go back to the reading passage about grasslands and underline the verbs written in the simple past tense and the present perfect tense. Write these sentences below. Then, using the guidelines for choosing between simple past and present perfect on page 123, write the rule that applies to each sentence.

Example: At one time the grassland *occupied* between 40 and
45 percent of the Earth's surface. *Rule 1b*

1.

2.

3.

4.

5.

6.

7.

8.

Simple Past and Present Perfect Tenses

The simple past tense is used to indicate an action or state that occurred in the past; the present perfect tense refers to an action or state in the past that continues up to (and perhaps beyond) the present. These two tenses are sometimes interchangeable with no change in meaning. The following discussion is a summary of when to use the simple past or when to use the present perfect.

Rule 1
a. Use the present perfect tense to describe an action that happened at an indefinite time in the past.

The world's population *has increased* dramatically, leading to more crop production in the grassland ecosystem.

b. Use the simple past for a specific time in the past.

When the world's population *increased* dramatically after the Industrial Revolution, there was an increase in crop production in the grassland ecosystem.

Rule 2
When the present perfect is used with *since* or *for,* it expresses an action, emotion, or event that started in the past and continues up to the present.
a. The simple past can never be used with *since.*

Correct: Farmers *have grown* crops in grasslands *since* the early 1800s.
Incorrect: Farmers *grew* crops in grasslands *since* the early 1800s.

b. The simple past can be used with *for,* but the meaning changes to imply that the activity is no longer true.

> *Correct:* Farmers *have grown* crops in grasslands *for* more than 150 years.
> *Correct with different meaning:* Farmers *grew* crops in grasslands *for* more than 150 years.

Rule 3
Use either the present perfect tense or the simple past tense with the words *just, already,* and *recently.*

> The prairie chicken *has recently been* listed as an endangered species.
> The prairie chicken *was recently* listed as an endangered species.

Rule 4
Use the present perfect tense in negative sentences with *yet* or *still.*

> Farmers *haven't developed* some areas of the grassland ecosystem for agriculture *yet.*

Rule 5
Use the present perfect tense of the verb *be* with frequency adverbs that imply that an action is repeated frequently. If you use the simple past tense, you imply that the meaning is no longer true.

> The prairie dog *has always been* good at mixing up the soil.
> The prairie dog *was always* good at mixing up the soil.

E. Edit these sentences for the correct use of simple past or present perfect tense. Not all of the sentences contain errors.

1. Nomads used the grassland for hundreds of years to herd their animals.

2. Africa just established a new game reserve to protect wild animals.

3. Man has destroyed much of the grassland in the world.

4. The bison didn't disappear yet.

5. Before he died, my grandfather has been a farmer for fifty years.

6. The lion was always good at hunting animals.

7. When they were alive, prairie dogs have competed with cattle for food.

F. Quickly skim the following paragraphs about animals that live in the grassland. Decide if the paragraph describes an example of mutualism, commensalism, or parasitism (see chap. 4).

1. During the dry season, elephants dig for water in sandy beds. When the elephants have finished drinking, many other kinds of animals come to drink the water.

2. The prairie dog destroyed the roots of certain shrubs. If these shrubs were left alive, they would have killed the grasses that the bison and antelope ate. The prairie dog benefited from the bison and antelope, because they trampled vegetation, allowing the prairie dog to see predators more easily.

III. Ecological Succession

A. In groups, discuss the following questions.

1. Where does an ecosystem come from? (In other words, does a tropical rain forest begin as a tropical rain forest?)
2. What are some disturbances that can hurt an ecosystem?
3. How many years does it take an ecosystem to recover after disturbance?

B. Read the following passage several times to make sure you understand the meaning of the terms *succession, climax ecosystem, primary succession,* and *secondary succession.*

> An ecosystem, such as a tropical rain forest, does not suddenly appear overnight. It develops over decades or centuries. Ecosystems mature just like people do, from infants to adults. An open field will eventually turn into a forest, but first it must go through several stages (temporary communities), similar to a human's developmental stages.
>
> This repeated replacement of communities over time is called *ecological succession.* It eventually ends in a *climax ecosystem,* which is the most mature and stable ecosystem possible for that area. It has a diversity of species and niches and can therefore tolerate stresses that would destroy a younger ecosystem. As a result, these mature ecosystems last for centuries if they are undisturbed.
>
> There are two types of succession: *primary succession* and *secondary succession.* During primary succession, a new ecosystem develops in an area where no organisms have lived before, like bare rocks after a retreating glacier, or lava that has cooled after a volcano. Secondary succession occurs where communities used to exist but were destroyed by a disturbance, such as a fire.

C. Now cover up the passage and write a definition for these terms **in your own words.** Do not look back at the passage!

succession:

climax ecosystem:

primary succession:

secondary succession:

D. Look at the following illustration and the accompanying descriptions of stages. These stages describe an instance of primary succession that occurred over the course of several hundred years following the retreat of a glacier. Read through the stages of primary succession, and underline all the words that signal a transition in time. After the description of stages, make a list of these words. Can you add any other words or expressions to this list?

Primary Succession (From G. Tyler Miller, Jr., *Living in the Environment* [Belmont, Calif.: 1979].)

Stage I—lichen community: After the glacier retreated, the bare rock was left without any life. Lichens began to colonize the rock. Lichens release chemicals that break down rock into small particles. These rock particles, along with the decaying material from dead lichens, formed soil. This soil held enough moisture and nutrients to support the second stage: mosses.

Stage II—moss community: After a while, the mosses crowded out the lichens. The mosses grew a little taller than the lichens, so they attracted insects and other animals, adding more organic material to the soil.

Stage III—plant community: At this point the soil had accumulated enough nutrients, organic matter, and moisture to support the growth of larger plants like goldenrods and asters. These plants attracted more insects and burrowing and grazing animals like moles and mice. If the climate had been a little drier, this stage would have contained mostly prairie grasses.

Stage IV—shrub community: Soon, taller woody shrubs, like wild rose and blackberry, became established due to the improved soil conditions. Deer, opossum, and red fox were successful in this shrub community.

Stage V—early tree stage community: Gradually, physical conditions (light, temperature, and moisture) changed. These new conditions made the soil even richer, which led to the next stage of succession: the early tree stage community. Squirrels and raccoons inhabited this early forest community.

Stage VI—climax forest: Finally, the soil was mature and soil conditions remained relatively constant. Moisture, light, nutrients, and temperature favored the growth of large trees.

Transitions:

E. Put the following paragraphs about secondary succession in order. Then rewrite the entire passage on a separate piece of paper, adding transitions of time where they are necessary and/or helpful.

The field is not bare for very long. Crabgrass, horseweed, and other weeds cover the ground. They grow because they are no longer kept under control by humans. These weeds are annual plants, which live only one season.

Hardwood species, such as maple and oak, grow under the pines. They grow taller than the pines. The pines die out in the shade. At least 200 years may be required for the development of this climax forest.

Often a forest is destroyed to make a field for growing crops. In order for plants to grow, people must constantly take care of the field. If it is left alone, however, this abandoned field will go through the stages of secondary succession.

More dead plants and debris accumulate. Decomposers build up the rich layer of soil needed for pine trees to grow. These trees shade out the perennials.

Organic material in the soil has built up. The soil can support perennials, like goldenrod, or broom sedge. The perennials shade out the weeds, so the weeds no longer survive.

F. Exchange papers from Activity E with a partner. Check to see if your partner has put the paragraphs in the proper order and used time transition signals correctly.

IV. Environmental Application: Global Warming

A climax community has diversity, and therefore stability. This mature, stable ecosystem contributes to the stability of the entire planet. Of course, we must keep some ecosystems in early successional stages in order for us to grow food, but we must be careful to maintain climax ecosystems as well.

We learned in chapter 3 that forests are often destroyed by logging, by clearing farmland, and by natural disturbances like fire. These trees play an important role in maintaining the climate of the earth. The removal of these trees, along with an increase in pollution during the last decade, has led to the environmental problem of *global warming*, sometimes called *the greenhouse effect.*

A. Imagine that you place two thermometers in the sun for ten minutes, but you cover one of the thermometers with a glass jar. Then, after ten minutes, you record the temperatures. What do you predict your data will tell you?

B. Read the following passage about global warming. Next to the appropriate paragraphs, put a *D* for the definition/description of the problem, a *C* for the cause(s) of the problem, an *E* for the effect(s) of the problem, and an *S* for the solution(s) to the problem.

The accumulation of certain gases in the earth's atmosphere has led to a warming of the earth's climate. Carbon dioxide and other gases act like a glass jar placed over the earth, in that they allow sunlight to pass through, but trap the heat inside. This process of trapping heat is very important, as it allows humans to live comfortably on the planet. Since the Industrial Revolution, however, atmospheric concentrations of these gases have increased, leading to an increase in the earth's temperature. Some climatologists predict that the earth may be, on average, warmer by 2 to 5 degrees Celsius by the year 2050.

If global temperatures rise, scientists predict that life on earth may face disastrous consequences. The change in climate will lead to more precipitation in some areas, causing flooding and erosion, and less precipitation in other areas, leading to crop failure and expanding deserts. When the polar ice cap melts, the sea level will rise. Rising seas could flood coastal areas. Finally, changes in habitat could lead to the extinction of plants and animals that are unable to adapt to the new conditions.

Carbon dioxide (CO_2)—the concentration of which is responsible for approximately half of the global warming trend—and nitrous oxide (N_2O) come from burning fossil fuels (coal, oil, gas). Although the United States has only 5 percent of the world's total population, it contributes 25 percent of the world's total carbon dioxide emissions. Deforestation, occurring at a rate of 27 million acres annually, also releases CO_2 that is stored in trees. In addition, we lose trees that are able to absorb CO_2 from the atmosphere during photosynthesis. A third greenhouse gas, methane, is produced by moist conditions with little oxygen, as in swamps, rice paddies, and landfills. Cattle also produce methane during digestion. Chlorofluorocarbons (CFCs), the fourth major greenhouse gas, are used in refrigerators and air conditioners, and in aerosol sprays in some countries.

People have responded to the threat of global warming in several ways. Some propose active solutions that would actually reduce the amount of carbon dioxide in the atmosphere. These solutions include spreading dust in the upper atmosphere to reflect sunlight, and adding iron to the ocean so that phytoplankton will increase, which would remove CO_2 from the atmosphere through photosynthesis. Others believe we should work to prevent any continued increase in greenhouse gases, through energy conservation measures and the slowing, or stopping, of deforestation.

C. Quickly scan the reading passage about global warming and find the following vocabulary words. Then match each word to its definition.

a. digestion   ___ place for garbage
b. accumulate   ___ to add to, give to
c. extinct   ___ to keep in
d. prediction   ___ to suggest
e. contribute   ___ a group of cows
f. adapt   ___ to let go
g. absorb   ___ process of wearing away
h. landfill   ___ to take in
i. cattle   ___ no longer existing
j. trap   ___ process by which food passes through the body
k. erosion
l. propose   ___ to collect
m. aerosol spray   ___ to change or adjust to new situation
n. release   ___ a guess about the future
     ___ liquid forced out (of a container) in the form of a fine mist

D. Look at the following sentence from the passage.

When the polar ice cap begins to melt, the sea level will rise.

Identify the two clauses in this sentence. Are they both independent clauses? What word connects these two clauses? What relationship is there between the two clauses?

Subordination with Adverbial Clauses

Subordination is used to link ideas of *unequal* importance. (Remember that in chapter 2 we learned about *coordination*, which links two independent clauses of *equal* importance.) In subordination, the less important idea is subordinated to the main idea. There are three types of subordinate clauses—adjectival (relative) clauses, adverbial clauses, and noun clauses. In this section, we will focus on subordination with adverbial clauses.

Adverbial clauses modify a verb, an adjective, or an adverb in a sentence. Like adverbs, they often answer the questions *why? when? where?* or *in what manner?*

The following list contains some of the subordinating conjunctions that introduce adverbial clauses, as well as their corresponding categories of meaning.

after (time)	if (condition)	unless (condition)
although (concession)	in order that (purpose)	until (time)
as (cause/time)	in that (purpose)	when (time)
because (cause)	provided that (condition)	whenever (time)
before (time)	since (cause/time)	where (place)
even if (concession)	so that (purpose)	wherever (place)
even though (concession)	though (concession)	while (time)

Too many short sentences in a paragraph can result in choppiness and can make your writing less interesting. You can make your writing more effective by showing the relative importance of ideas through subordination.

E. Find the sentences in the reading passage about global warming with adverbial clauses and write the sentences in the following spaces. Circle the subordinating conjunction used in the sentence.

> *Example:* Carbon dioxide and other gases act like a glass jar placed over the earth, (in that) they allow sunlight to pass through, but trap the heat inside.

1.

2.

3.

4.

5.

F. Insert an appropriate subordinating conjunction in the blank spaces in the following sentences.

1. Environmental problems have become worse _____ the Industrial Revolution.

2. _____ the amount of greenhouse gases are reduced, global warming may lead to disastrous consequences.

3. _____ aerosols have been banned in the United States for many years, they are still found in some developing countries.

4. The developing countries will reduce their use of fossil fuels _____ the industrial nations help them financially.

5. _____ the population continues to grow, the consumption of fossil fuel energy increases.

6. Adding iron to the ocean may help the global warming problem _____ the iron increases phytoplankton, which in turn promotes photosynthesis.

7. _____ cattle digest their food, they release methane.

8. Deforestation contributes to the greenhouse effect _____

   _____ the trees release CO_2 _____ they are burned.

G. Use the information you learned about the causes and effects of global warming to make a list of at least five possible solutions to the problem. Think carefully and be as specific as you can.

References

Speth, Gus. *Fact Sheet on Global Warming.* Stanford, CA: Earth Day, 1990.

Kunzig, Robert. "Earth on Ice," *Discover,* April, 1991: 55–61.

Houghton, Richard A., and George M. Woodell. "Global Climatic Change," *Scientific American,* April 1989: 36–44.

V. Environmental Application 2: Desertification

A. In the past 50 years, the advancing desert has swallowed 160 million acres of land in Africa alone. This process of an advancing desert is known as *desertification,* and it is an environmental threat to the grassland ecosystem. Read the following definition of desertification.

> Desertification is the irreversible decline of the biological productivity of arid and semiarid land resulting from pressures caused by too many people and abiotic factors.

Now read a different definition below. Does this definition say the same thing? How is this definition different?

> When arid and semiarid lands lose their ability to support life forever, it is called desertification. Desertification is caused by overpopulation and physical factors.

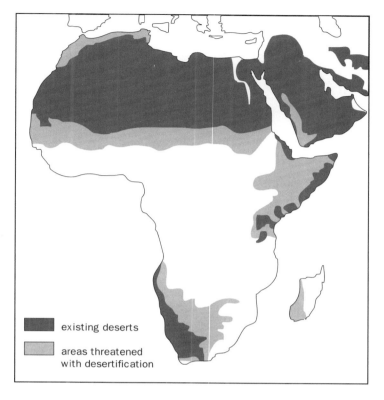

Desertification in Africa

Paraphrasing

Paraphrasing is a process by which writers express someone else's meaning in their own words. Paraphrasing is a very helpful tool when you are trying to remember new concepts or vocabulary words that are difficult; it is much easier to remember them if you can say them in your own words!

Paraphrasing other people's words and ideas is a very difficult skill to master. First, you must not only understand the original meaning, but you must also rewrite the language while keeping the original meaning. Paraphrasing requires a great deal of practice and skill.

How to Paraphrase

1. Read the passage very carefully to make sure you understand the meaning.
2. Put the material aside, and then write in your own words what you remember.
3. Check your writing against the original by rereading the passage to make sure you have:
   a. conveyed the same meaning
   b. kept your paraphrase about the same length
   c. written the paraphrase in your own style of writing

Techniques for Paraphrasing

1. Change the *grammatical structure* by:
   a. joining short sentences or breaking up long ones
   b. changing active verbs to passive verbs and vice-versa
   c. changing the word order, especially of adverbs
2. Change the *vocabulary* to more common synonyms and expressions and simpler phrases. However, you should *not* change technical vocabulary (desertification), proper names (Earth Summit), and numbers or statistics (50%, 1990).

B. Read the following paragraphs about the causes of desertification. Then paraphrase them *in your own words.*

1. Wind and rain can damage the land. Wind picks up the fertile topsoil and blows it away. Soil is washed away by rain. This process is called erosion. Once the topsoil disappears, it cannot be replaced.

_____

_____

_____

2. People chop down trees for fuelwood, for building material, and to clear farmland. Soon no trees are left to shade the ground or hold the soil in place. The soil blows away, leaving a barren land.

    _____

    _____

    _____

3. Desertification of the land is also caused by drought. In the 1930s, a long drought turned parts of the Great Plains of North America into "the Dust Bowl." The topsoil blew away in terrible dust storms, and nothing could grow.

    _____

    _____

    _____

4. The nomads herd cows, goats, or sheep from one place to another. When these animals eat so much grass that it cannot grow back, it is called overgrazing. In addition, the trampling hooves of the animals pack down the earth so no seeds can sprout.

    _____

    _____

    _____

5. Cash crop farming helped desertification of the Sahel, an area in northern Africa. In the past, farmers had planted only enough to feed their families. But during the heavy rains in the 1960s, they planted huge crops of cotton and peanuts to sell. These crops used up all the nutrients in the soil and made the fields useless. When the farmers abandoned their land, the topsoil blew away.

    _____

_____

_____

C. Although some land has been irreversibly harmed, many scientists feel that much of the land classified as desertified is really in a state of degradation, which can be reversed by adopting certain measures. On the left side of the following chart, summarize the causes of desertification from Activity B. Then think about some things that could lessen the effects of these causes and write them on the right side of the chart. An example is provided.

Causes	Solutions
1. Agriculture	a. Farmers could use contour plowing, whereby they don't plant in straight lines, but instead follow the dips and curves of the land. Therefore, the wind does not blow the topsoil away. b. Farmers shouldn't grow so many crops that they take away all the nutrients in the soil.

References

Dodd, Jerrold L. "Desertification and Degradation in Sub-Saharan Africa." *BioScience,* Jan. 1994: 28–33.

Hinrichsen, Don. "Kenya's Arid Lands: Rising from the Dust." *International Wildlife,* May-June 1992: 12–23.

Hogan, Paula. *Expanding Deserts.* Milwaukee: Gareth Stevens Children's Books, 1991.

Chapter 7

The Desert Ecosystem

Read the following statements. Write a *T* if you think the statement is true, or an *F* if you think it is false. As you study this chapter, you will discover whether these statements are true or false. When you finish the chapter, return to this page and check your answers to see if they are right.

1. ___ The highest temperature ever recorded in a desert was 114°F.

2. ___ A true desert receives less than ten inches of precipitation per year.

3. ___ One type of cactus can grow 30 to 40 feet high.

4. ___ It can snow in the desert.

5. ___ The largest desert is the Gobi Desert in Mongolia.

6. ___ Most animals in the desert are active during the day.

7. ___ Some desert animals never drink water.

A Look Behind/A Look Ahead

In the last chapter we studied the physical features and the plants and animals of the grassland ecosystem. We learned that ecosystems are constantly changing, yet they maintain relative stability over time. Succession is an example of how an ecosystem returns to stability after a disturbance. Finally, we analyzed the causes, effects, and possible solutions related to global warming.

This chapter will cover the desert ecosystems of the world and their typical characteristics. We will learn about the adaptations animals and plants have for living in the extreme conditions of this ecosystem. We will then apply this knowledge in our study of the environmental problem of endangered species.

To the Student

After completing this chapter, you will be able to:

1. name and locate the major deserts of the world.
2. state a few basic facts about the size, average temperatures, and precipitation amounts for the major deserts of the world.
3. describe several plants and animals and their adaptations to life in the desert.
4. explain how animals become endangered, choose and defend an argument for or against saving endangered species, and propose individual solutions to the problem.

After completing this chapter, return to this page and assess your own achievement in reaching these goals.

Vocabulary Development

Throughout this book, we have learned about the pronunciation and grammar (i.e., the part of speech) of words in English. In addition, we have learned certain strategies for guessing the meaning of words we don't know, by looking at the word's morphology and the surrounding context. We have also studied how to use a dictionary to discover more about the pronunciations, grammar, and meanings of vocabulary words.

You have been introduced to many new vocabulary words in this textbook. What is the best way to remember all of these new words? Well, researchers in second language acquisition believe that people will remember vocabulary better if it is presented in a contextualized and meaningful way, and if it is recycled, or reused, again and again. All of the vocabulary you learned in this text was essential for understanding the larger picture of ecology, and most of the important words were recycled throughout the chapters. This method of presentation should help you retain the new words you learned in this book, but you will also probably need to do some extra studying of any new vocabulary words. Making and studying vocabulary cards are useful tools to help you remember words. Look at this example of a vocabulary card.

adapt (v) to change or adjust to new situation; adaptation (n); adaptable (adj.)

Kangaroo rats have *adapted* to life in the desert by obtaining the water they need through the digestion of food.

You do not need to follow the format of this card exactly; write out the information about a vocabulary word in a way that is helpful to you. It is very important, however, that you use the vocabulary word in a sentence that makes sense to you. Study these vocabulary cards whenever you have any free time: riding on a bus, waiting for an appointment, or just before you go to sleep. As you encounter new words that are important to you in this chapter, make vocabulary cards for these words and study them often.

I. Deserts of the World

A. Look at the following map showing the major deserts of the world. Listen to the speaker carefully and fill in the desert name on the list next to the number to which it corresponds. Some of the answers have been given to you. The names of the deserts are listed before the map to help you spell them.

Sahara	Kalahari	Namib	Turkestan	Thar
Mojave	Atacama	Sonoran	Patagonian	Great Basin
Simpson	Gibson	Arabian	Iranian	Great Sandy

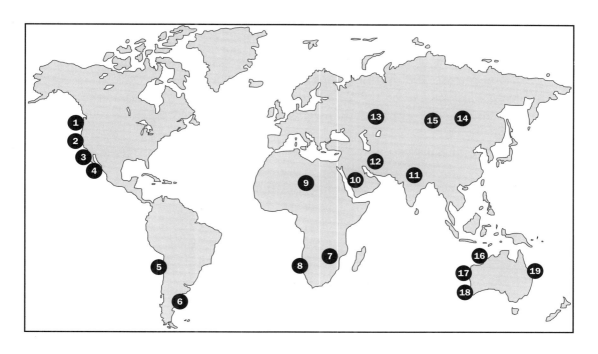

1.	6.	11.	16.
2.	7.	12.	17.
3.	8.	13.	18. Great Victoria
4. Chihuahuan	9.	14. Gobi	19.
5.	10.	15. Takla Makan	

B. Look at the following sentences from the listening passage.

The Iranian Desert is *between* the Arabian Desert and the Thar Desert of India.

The Atacama Desert is *across from* the Patagonian Desert.

What part of speech are the italicized words?

Prepositions of Space

A preposition is a word that shows a connection between the noun at the end of a phrase and another word in the sentence.

Prepositions can be separated into two basic categories: prepositions of time and space, and prepositions that show logical relationships between things.

In the passage you just heard, the speaker used many prepositions of space.

The following list represents prepositions of space:

above	across	against	along	among
around	at	away from	before	behind
below	beneath	beside	between	beyond
by	down	far (away) from	from	as (far) as
in	in back of	in front of	inside	inside of
in the middle of	into	near	next to	off
on	opposite	out	out of	outside
over	past	round	through	throughout
to	towards	under	underneath	up

C. Write a correct sentence about the location of each desert named in the following list. Use your map from Activity A to help you. An example sentence has been done for you.

Example: Namib

The Namib lies *along* the Atlantic Ocean.

1. the Great Sandy Desert

2. the Atacama Desert

3. the Sahara Desert

4. the Thar Desert

5. the Chihuahuan Desert

II. Physical Features of the Desert

A. The following passage describes some of the physical features of deserts. After reading a few sentences, you will be asked to make a prediction about what you think will come next in the passage. Cover the page below each stop sign to avoid seeing the answers.

Deserts are land areas where more water is lost through evaporation than is gained through precipitation. An area is described as a desert if ten inches or less of rain falls each year.

Deserts are categorized into five types depending on their climates.

I expect the next part of the passage to talk about:

The five types of deserts are called *subtropical, cool coastal* (Namib and Atacama), *rain shadow* (North American deserts), *interior continental* (Sahara, Arabian, Iranian), and *polar.* The first four of these types of deserts enjoy warm or hot summers and relatively cool winters. Water is lacking throughout most of the year.

I expect the next part of the passage to talk about:

In polar deserts the brief summers are generally cool or cold, and the winter is very cold. Water is present but usually frozen, so it is not available to the plants and animals.

The greatest limiting factors for plants and animals in a hot desert are water and heat.

I expect the next part of the passage to talk about:

Rain does not come frequently or regularly. Months or years can pass before there is a storm. One section of the Sahara Desert went without rain for 11 years! When the storms do come, they are often very violent, leading to flooding and erosion.

The dryness is also responsible for the high temperatures in the hot deserts.

I expect the next part of the passage to talk about:

Usually, moisture in the air forms a blanket that protects the earth from the sun's rays. Lacking this blanket of moisture, the desert heats up rapidly during the day and cools off rapidly at night. Therefore, the temperature range in a desert from morning to night can be as much as 50°F. The hottest temperature ever recorded in the desert was 136.4°F in the Sahara.

B. How does making predictions while reading a passage or listening to a lecture help improve your English?

C. Now read the entire passage again and answer the following questions.

    1. What is the hottest temperature ever recorded in a desert?

    2. What are the two main limiting factors in the desert ecosystem?

    3. How does the lack of moisture create heat in the desert?

    4. What is the definition of a desert?

    5. What are the five types of deserts?

D. The following table provides information about the size, annual precipitation, and the maximum and minimum temperatures for each of the major deserts of the world.

Deserts of the World

desert name (location)	area		mean annual precipitation		temperature in F (C)	
	sq mi	sq km	in.	mm	maximum	minimum
Africa						
Sahara (northern Africa)	3,320,000	8,600,000	8	200	109 (43)	50 (10)
Kalahari (SW Africa)	100,000	260,000	8-26	200-660	117 (47)	8 (-13)
Namib (SW Africa)	52,000	135,000	—	—	—	—
North America						
Great Basin (southwestern US)	190,000	492,000	10	250	—	—
Chihuahuan (northern Mexico)	175,000	450,000	—	—	—	—
Sonoran (southwestern US)	120,000	310,000	7	180	118 (48)	17 (-8)
Mojave (southwestern US)	25,000	65,000	5	130	117 (47)	7 (-14)
South America						
Patagonian (southern Argentina)	260,000	673,000	3.5-17	90-430	113 (45)	12 (-1)
Atacama (northern Chile)	54,000	140,000	3	75	—	—
Asia						
Arabian (southwestern Asia)	900,000	2,330,000	4	100	124 (51)	154 (12)
Gobi (northern China)	500,000	1,300,000	3-8	70-200	113 (45)	-40 (-40)
Takla Makan (northern China)	105,000	270,000	.4-1.5	10-38	100 (38)	-4 (-20)
Turkestan (SW Russia)	750,000	1,875,000	—	—	—	—
Iranian (Iran)	150,000	375,000	—	—	—	—
Thar (India and Pakistan)	230,000	575,000	4-20	100-500	122 (50)	41 (5)
Australia						
Great Victoria (SW Australia)	250,000	650,000	—	—	—	—
Great Sandy (NW Australia)	150,000	400,000	—	—	—	—
Gibson (western Australia)	—	—	—	—	—	—
Simpson (Northern Territory)	56,000	145,000	—	—	—	—

Adapted from *Encyclopædia Britannica*, 15th ed. (Chicago: *Encyclopædia Britannica*, 1988).

Using your knowledge of comparatives and superlatives from chapter 4, write at least five sentences about the information. Use a variety of adjectives and adverbs like hot, dry, rainy, small, etc. An example sentence has been written for you.

Example: The Sahara is the largest desert in the world.

III. Adaptations of Life in the Desert

In order to live with the lack of water and the extreme temperatures in the desert, plants and animals have two basic mechanisms for survival: they can either escape, or they can endure by adapting to the conditions.

A. In Activities B and D, we will look at several paragraphs describing adaptations desert plants and animals have for enduring the extreme temperatures and lack of water. Look at the following headings for the paragraphs. What adaptation do you think the paragraph will discuss, based on the words in the heading? Can you describe how the adaptation enables the plant or animal to survive?

Roots Dig Deep   *Reptiles Move with the Sun*

Snake Sidesteps the Desert Heat   *Leaves Die so Plants Can Live*

Large Ears Aren't Only for Hearing

B. Match each of the following paragraphs about *plants* and their adaptations to the appropriate picture.

___ Nature's Water Tower
A type of cactus called the saguaro is found in the Sonoran Desert and can grow as tall as 30 to 40 feet. The trunk and branches of the saguaro expand and contract. When it rains, the trunk and branches expand and the saguaro can store hundreds of gallons of water.

___ Roots Dig Deep
The North American mesquite tree grows long roots that can get moisture at depths of 50 to 175 feet below the surface of the ground.

__ Leaves Die So Plants Can Live
Since leaves lose a great deal of water through evaporation, most plants in the desert are leafless. Other plants, like the ocotillo, lose their leaves when there is little rain.

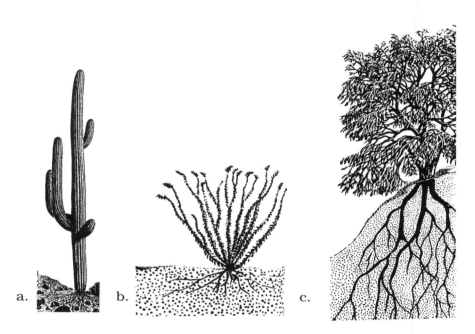

a.   b.   c.

C. Summarize, in your own words, the adaptations plants have for surviving in the desert:

D. Now read the following paragraphs about the adaptations of desert animals.

A Long Hike
The larger mammals of the desert, like antelopes and wild asses, are able to travel long distances to get water.

wild ass

Specialized Feathers Soak Up Water
The African, and the Asian sandgrouse, both fly to water each morning to dip their breast feathers in it. These feathers soak up water like sponges. The birds then fly back to their young, and the young drink the water from the wet feathers.

Taking a Nap
During periods of extreme heat and drought, some animals, like the pocket mouse, will hibernate.

pocket mouse

Hot Pads
Camels have thick pads on the bottoms of their feet so they can walk without discomfort on the hot sand.

camel

Scales Prevent Water Loss
The scales of reptiles like the gecko help prevent evaporation and resist drying.

gecko

Snake Sidesteps the Desert Heat
The sidewinder rattlesnake of North America has developed an efficient way to move over hot desert sand. It pushes its body forward in a sideways S motion, with only two parts of the snake's body touching the ground at any given time.

Rodents That Don't Drink
The kangaroo rat, like the
jerboa in the Middle East
and the gerbil in Africa,
makes its own water by
eating dry seeds and turn-
ing these seeds into water
in its body. These rodents
(kangaroo rat, jerboa, and
gerbil) may never take a
drink of water in their life.
They don't need to: they
make their own.

fennec fox   jerboa

Large Ears Aren't Only for Hearing
The jackrabbit of North America and the carnivorous fennec fox of
the Sahara use their big ears to give off body heat to cool themselves
down.

Flying High
Vultures, hawks, and fal-
cons conserve energy and
stay cool by gliding in the
cool air 3000 feet or more
above the ground.

hawk

Reptiles Move with the Sun
Like all reptiles, the spiny
lizard assumes the tem-
perature of its environ-
ment. It can regulate its
body temperature by mov-
ing between sun and
shade during the day, and
by becoming more active
at night and in the early
morning.

spiny lizard

Digging for a Drink
The collared peccary digs
into the earth to eat the
moist roots of cacti and
other plants.

collared peccary

E. Fill in the following chart by writing the name of each animal and the adaptation it has for surviving extreme heat or lack of water. Part of the chart has been completed for you.

Type of Animal	Animal Name	Heat	Animal Name	Lack of Water
Reptile	1. sidewinder snake 2.	moves sideways	1.	
Bird	1.		1.	
Rodent	1.		1. kangaroo rat, jerboa, gerbil	makes water from digestion of seeds
Small Mammal	1.		1.	
Large Mammal	1.		1.	

F. With a partner, create an imaginary plant or animal that is especially well adapted to the desert environment. Describe what it would look like and the characteristics it would have. Give this new plant or animal a name and share your idea with the rest of the class.

IV. Environmental Application: Endangered Species

A. We just learned about several adaptations plants and animals have for survival. If a species is unable to adapt to environmental changes, it will disappear, or become *extinct.*

Read this quote and answer the questions that follow.

> Man depends on wildlife for survival, and wildlife depends equally on man. The two must find means for living together on earth or there will be no life on earth.

(Raymond R. Dasman, "Wildlife and Ecosystems," *Wildlife and America: Contributions to an Understanding of American Wildlife and its Conservation* (GPO, Council on Environmental Quality, 1978, 18)

Using the knowledge you have gained in this book, what do you think this quote means? Why?

B. Quickly skim through the following passage, *Saving the Wildlife*, by reading the first sentence of each paragraph and by looking at any words that are printed in italics, any charts, and any pictures. Without looking back at the passage, write down some of the main ideas.

C. Now read the entire passage. As you read it, underline any vocabulary words you don't know. *Do not* look them up in a dictionary; simply underline them.

SAVING THE WILDLIFE

Of the estimated 500 million species of plants and animals that have existed since life began on earth, only 2 million are confirmed here today. In the 1990s, scientists expect at least one species will vanish every hour. Although extinction is a natural evolutionary process, the increase in the human population during recent decades has caused a rapid and unnatural increase in the rate of extinction.

Wild animals (as well as plants) that are heading toward extinction are listed in *The Red Data Book*, which is published by the International Union for the Conservation of Nature and Natural Resources (IUCN). These species are categorized according to seven degrees of endangerment: extinct, rare, endangered, threatened, vulnerable, indeterminate, and insufficiently known. Animals are categorized as *extinct* if they have not been identified in the wild in the past fifty years. The remaining categories of *rare, endangered, threatened,* or *vulnerable* all run the risk of becoming extinct if the factors that put them at risk continue to affect them. Finally, species are categorized as *indeterminate* or *insufficiently known* if they are considered to be at risk but there is not enough information available to place them in a more appropriate category.

Scientists believe that there could be millions of different species of unnamed animals now living on earth, so why should we care if some of these become extinct? One reason is the aesthetic value that wildlife provides. The beauty of animals provides many people with enjoyment—through hobbies such as bird watching, or photography, or simply through visiting a zoo or wildlife refuge to gaze at these creatures.

Many wild animals also have a cultural value to humans. Some races view certain animals as objects of worship, and many folk tales and children's stories are based on animals. Animals have also influenced the culture of language with expressions like "wise as an owl." Furthermore, animals are used as national symbols, such as the Russian bear and the bald eagle in the United States.

The economic benefits of medicines, food, and material resources that come from wild animals are enormous. Many important medicines are derived from animals, such as venom from the Malayan pit viper that is used to prevent the formation of blood clots. Biomedical research also relies on certain wild species, such as the rhesus monkey, used in the development of the polio vaccine.

No greater benefit is received from other organisms than the daily nourishment we get from them. Most of our food today comes from domesticated animals, but all of these species derived from wild species. And wild species, especially marine animals, still support many people in different parts of the world today. We not only receive food from wild animals, but also materials such as silk, leather, oils, down, fur, and ivory for manufactured products.

However, the biological value wild species possess may be the most important argument for preserving them. Every species is a link in the chain of life; every living thing potentially affects every other living thing and the physical environment of this planet. If you take away one block of the "pyramid of life," it might not fall down. But if you remove hundreds or even thousands of blocks, the pyramid will certainly fall down. And remember, humans will fall with that pyramid.

Finally, there is an ethical argument to make when speaking of endangered species. Humans share the earth with all living creatures, and we should recognize that they too have a right to exist.

In order to prevent the extinction of animals, we must look at why and how they are threatened. The following chart summarizes the human causes of species extinction. Most species, however, do not become extinct from a single cause but by a combination of factors.

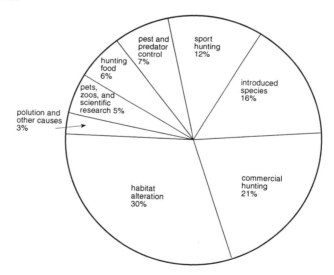

Human Causes of Extinction (From G. Tyler Miller, Jr., *Living in the Environment* [Belmont, Calif.: Wadsworth, 1979].)

The most important cause of extinction and the greatest threat to wildlife is the destruction or alteration of habitat. Habitat damage can occur through the cutting and clearing of forests for development or agriculture, the conversion of grassland to agriculture, overgrazing, mining, pollutants, and the development of recreational areas, highways, dams, airports, and cities.

Animals also become endangered through overhunting, or the killing of animals faster than they can reproduce. Commercial hunting involves the killing of animals for various products that will be traded internationally, such as furs, tusks, feathers, etc. The profits from the world trade of these luxury goods—or in live trade for zoos, pets, or scientific research—is estimated at a minimum of 5 billion dollars annually.

Another cause of species endangerment, introducing new species into an ecosystem, can have unpredictable and sometimes harmful effects on the ecosystem. Introduced species can threaten naturally established species by preying on them, competing with them for food, or destroying their habitat.

Unwanted pests and predators (mostly of domestic livestock) are killed through hunting or poisoning. Removing a predator from the food chain may also lead to endangerment of animals further down the food chain because of the important role a predator plays in an ecosystem.

Pollution can not only destroy the habitat, but it can have a direct effect on the wild animals themselves. Oil spills, pesticides, and industrial wastes are just some of the poisonous substances that can harm wildlife.

It's too late to save the animals that are already extinct, but there is still hope for those that are endangered. Endangered species are protected by the Endangered Species Act, a federal law passed by the United States Congress in 1973. The purpose of this act is to protect endangered species from being killed or injured, from being illegally traded, or from having their habitats destroyed. It prohibits the federal government from funding any activities, such as building dams or logging, that would harm a listed species or reduce its chance of survival. The Act does not prevent private development, however.

On an international level, endangered species are protected by the Conventional International Trade in Endangered Species of Wild Fauna and Flora (CITES) agreement, of which 99 countries are signers. This agreement prohibits international trade, or requires import and export permits for trade, depending on the category of the endangered species in question.

Another way that endangered species can be protected is through the establishment and management of wildlife refuges and game reserves. Animals can also be protected in zoos, and captive breeding programs can be developed to try to increase the numbers of certain animals. Some of the animals that have been raised in captivity can then be released to the wild, in an attempt to re-establish a natural population.

People must begin to place a value on species diversity and realize the incredible link that exists between all living and nonliving things, humans included. We must realize that we are no more immune to the slow destruction of the planet than is the bald eagle, or the Bengal tiger, or the Grevy's zebra.

D. Answer the following questions about the organization of the passage.

1. What paragraph serves as the introduction to the passage?

2. What is the first main idea presented in the passage and what support does the writer use for this idea?

3. What is the second main idea and its support?

4. What is the third main idea and its support?

5. What is the fourth main idea and its support?

6. What paragraph serves as the conclusion for the passage?

E. Write the topic sentence for each main idea in the reading passage.

F. Choose some of the words in the passage that you underlined in Activity C. First, write the sentence that contains the vocabulary word. Next, decide which strategy you will use for that vocabulary word from the following guidelines. If you cannot ignore the word, write the definition in the space provided. Two examples have been done for you.

Summary of Vocabulary Strategies

The following strategies can be used when you are confronted with a vocabulary word you do not know.

1. ignore the word
2. guess the meaning from the surrounding context
3. guess the meaning from the word's morphology
4. use a dictionary

Always begin with number 1. If you can ignore the word, then *do so.* If the word, however, is necessary to understand the meaning of the sentence, then use one or more of the remaining strategies. Try to become less dependent on your dictionary, as constantly looking up words slows your reading down.

Example:

Of the *estimated* 500 million species of plants and animals . . .
> *Strategy:* 1—I can ignore this word and still understand the sentence.
> *Definition:* (a definition is not needed)

One reason is the *aesthetic* value that wildlife provides. The beauty of animals provides many people with enjoyment—through hobbies such as bird watching, or photography . . .
> *Strategy:* 3—guess from surrounding context
> *Definition:* beauty

1. _____

   _____

   Strategy:
   Definition:

2. _____

_____

Strategy:
Definition:

3. _____

_____

Strategy:
Definition:

4. _____

_____

Strategy:
Definition:

5. _____

_____

Strategy:
Definition:

6. _____

_____

Strategy:
Definition:

7. _____

_____

Strategy:
Definition:

8. _____

_____

Strategy:
Definition:

G. The reading passage details several arguments for saving endangered species. Many people, however, argue that we shouldn't do anything. Below is a list of counterarguments, arguments *against* saving endangered species. Read the arguments, and write a statement that refutes the argument, or shows that the argument is incorrect. Use the information from the reading passage. An example is provided.

Example:

Counterargument: Opponents of saving endangered species argue that species extinction is part of the natural course of development of life on earth.
Refutation: Humans have increased the rate of extinction far beyond the natural course of development. In fact, scientists say that currently at least one species becomes extinct every hour.

1. *Counterargument:* Most of the endangered species aren't exciting animals, like lions and tigers, but useless and uninteresting animals.
   Refutation:

2. *Counterargument:* The world won't change dramatically if we lose a few animals here and there.
   Refutation:

H. Choose a side to this argument and write an argumentative essay on a separate piece of paper.

Argumentative Essays

The following provides two organizational plans for an argumentative essay. Either format is fine; choose one that matches your purpose, your topic, and your audience.

Option One
 I. Introduction
 II. Background paragraph about the topic
 III. Pro argument 1*
 IV. Pro argument 2
 V. Pro argument 3
 VI. Counterarguments and refutations
 VII. Conclusion

Option Two
 I. Introduction
 II. Background paragraph about the topic
 III. Counterargument 1 and pro argument to refute it*
 IV. Counterargument 2 and pro argument to refute it
 V. Counterargument 3 and pro argument to refute it
 VI. Conclusion

 *Some writers think it is better to put your weakest argument first and build to your strongest argument.

I. Review the causes of extinction in the reading "Saving the Wildlife." Match each of the following descriptions to its appropriate cause. An example has been done for you.

Example: When crews started to build the Union Pacific Railroad in 1865, thousands of bison were killed to supply the construction workers with meat. "Buffalo Bill" Cody bragged of killing 4,280 bison in eighteen months. In less than twenty years, the bison were close to extinction.

Hunting for food

1. Before Europeans came to Hawaii, there were no animals there that preyed on birds. For this reason, many types of Hawaiian birds

could safely build their nests on the ground. However, European ships accidentally introduced rats to the islands. The rats started eating the eggs of the ground-nesting birds. People brought in mongooses to combat the rats, but the mongooses ate more bird eggs instead.

2. Some people grind the horns of rhinos into a powder that they say can cure high fevers. Others use the horns for decorative objects. Rhino horns sell for approximately $6,000 per pound.

3. An infestation of the Levant vole, a mouse-like animal, occurred in 1975–76 in the northern Huleh Valley of Israel, which caused serious damage to alfalfa fields. Farmers sprayed Azodrin, a pesticide, to kill the voles.

4. The pesticide not only killed the voles, it also killed about four hundred of the Middle East's thin supply of eagles, hawks, owls, and other predatory birds that fed on the voles.

5. The subtropical forest habitat of a small cat in Japan called the Iriomote cat, first named in the 1960s, is being cleared for pineapple, sugarcane, and other crops. It is possible that the Iriomote cat will set a modern record for mammals—less than forty years from first description to final extinction.

J. The reading passage mentions several possible means of preserving endangered species. Make a list of some things you can do on *an individual level* to help protect endangered plants and animals.

References

Anderson, Robert. *Endangered Species: Understanding Words in Context.* San Diego: Greenhaven Press, 1991.

DiSilvestro, Roger. *The Endangered Kingdom: The Struggle to Save America's Wildlife.* New York: John Wiley and Sons, 1989.

Erlich, Paul, and Anne Erlich. *Extinction.* New York: Random House, 1981.

Facklam, Margery. *And Then There Was One: The Mysteries of Extinction.* San Francisco: Sierra Club Books, 1990.

Fitzgerald, Sarah. *International Wildlife Trade: Whose Business Is It?* Washington, DC: World Wildlife Fund, 1989.

Nilsson, Greta. *The Endangered Species Handbook.* Washington, DC: Animal Welfare Institute, 1983.

Schwartz, Linda. *Earth Book for Kids.* Santa Barbara: The Learning Works, 1990.

Wexo, John Bonnett. *Endangered Animals.* Mankato, MN: Creative Education, 1987.

Appendixes

Measurement Units

Length

U.S. Unit	U.S. Equivalents	Metric Equivalents
inch	—	2.54 centimeters
foot	12 inches	0.3048 meter
yard	3 feet, or 36 inches	0.9144 meter
mile	5, 280 feet	1.61 kilometers

Area

U.S. Unit	U.S. Equivalents	Metric Equivalents
square mile	640 acres	2,590 square kilometers

Volume or Capacity

U.S. Unit	U.S. Equivalents	Metric Equivalents
pint	16 ounces	0.473 liter
quart	2 pints	0.946 liter
gallon	4 quarts	3.785 liters

Weight

U.S. Unit	U.S. Equivalents	Metric Equivalents
pound	16 ounces	453.59237 grams
ton	2,000 pounds	0.907 metric ton

Appendix B

Glossary

Abiotic nonliving

Abyssal zone bottom zone of the ocean

Adapt change in order to survive in different surroundings

Albedo a measure of the reflectivity of the earth and its atmosphere

Alga (algae) simple one-celled or many-celled plant, usually aquatic, capable of carrying on photosynthesis

Annual a plant whose entire life span is in one growing season

Atmosphere the gaseous envelope of air surrounding the earth

Atoms extremely small particles that are the basic building blocks of all matter

Autotrophic organism an organism that uses solar energy to photosynthesize organic food substances and other organic chemicals from carbon dioxide and water; compare to *heterotrophic organism*

Bacteria smallest living organisms; with fungi, they comprise the decomposer level of the food chain

Biome a large terrestrial ecosystem characterized by distinct types of plants and animals and maintained under the climatic conditions of the region

Biosphere sum total of all the various ecosystems on the planet along with their interactions; the sphere of air, water, and land in which all life is found

Biotic living

Biotic (reproductive) potential the maximum rate at which a population can reproduce with unlimited resources and ideal environmental conditions

Carbon dioxide (CO_2) a gas formed of a combination of one atom of carbon and two atoms of oxygen; an important part of the atmosphere

Carnivore meat-eating organism

170

Carrying capacity maximum population that a given ecosystem can support indefinitely under a given set of environmental conditions

Chlorofluorocarbons (CFCs) human-made gases combining chlorine, fluorine, and carbon; widely used in refrigerators and air conditioners; contributes to ozone destruction and global warming

Chlorophyll the green pigment that allows plants to make food from sunlight

Climate the average of daily atmospheric conditions (weather) over a relatively long period of time

Climax ecosystem (climax community) a relatively stable stage of ecological succession; a mature ecosystem with a diverse array of species and ecological niches, capable of using energy and cycling critical chemicals more efficiently than simpler, immature ecosystems

Commensalism a symbiotic relationship between two different species in which one species benefits from the association while the other is apparently neither helped nor harmed; see *mutualism, parasitism, symbiosis*

Community (natural) group of plant and animal populations living and interacting in a given locality

Competition two or more species in the same ecosystem attempting to use the same scarce resources

Consumer organism that lives off other organisms, generally divided into primary consumers (herbivores), secondary consumers (carnivores), and microconsumers (decomposers)

Decomposer an organism such as bacterium or fungus that feeds upon and breaks down dead organic matter

Deforestation clearing of forests by cutting or burning

Density the size of the population in a particular unit of space

Desert an arid ecosystem characterized by little moisture, extreme temperatures, and low diversity

Desertification the process that converts grasslands or forests to deserts

Developed nation nation that, compared with less industrialized nations, typically has (1) a high average per capita income, (2) a low rate of population growth, (3) a small fraction of its labor force employed in agriculture, (4) a low level of adult illiteracy, and (5) a strong economy

Developing nation nation that, compared with more industrialized nations, typically has (1) a low average per capita income, (2) a high rate of population growth, (3) a large fraction of its labor force employed in agriculture, (4) a high level of adult illiteracy, and (5) a weak economy and financial base because only a few items are available for export

Diversity physical or biological complexity of a system; in many cases it leads to an ecosystem's stability

Drought a long period when no rain falls

Ecosystem self-sustaining and self-regulating community of organisms interacting with one another and with their environment

Endangered species species in immediate danger of biological extinction or extermination

Energy ability or capacity to do work by pushing or pulling some form of matter

Energy flow in ecology, the one-way transfer of energy through an ecosystem; the way in which energy is converted and expended at each trophic level

Energy (food) pyramid figure representing the loss or degradation of useful energy at each step of the food chain; about 80 to 90 percent of the energy in each transfer is lost as waste heat, and the resulting shape of the energy levels is that of a pyramid

Environment aggregate of external conditions that influence the life of an individual organism or population

Erosion the wearing away of a substance; soil is worn away by water and wind

Extinction complete disappearance of a species

Extrinsic limiting factor factor that can regulate population growth and size by operating from outside a population; examples are food supply, climate, and disease; compare *intrinsic limiting factor*

Food chain sequence of transfers of energy in the form of food from organisms in one trophic level to those in another when one organism eats or decomposes another

Food web complex, interlocking series of food chains

Fossil fuel remains of dead plants and animals of a previous geologic area that can be burned to release energy; examples are coal, oil, and natural gas

Gaseous cycle biogeochemical cycle with the atmosphere as the primary reservoir; examples include the oxygen and nitrogen cycles

Global warming trapping of heat in the atmosphere

Glucose a simple form of sugar made by plants during photosynthesis

Grasslands a treeless, grassy, plains ecosystem found in North America, Eurasia, and Australia

Groundwater water beneath the surface of the ground

Habitat place where an organism or community of organisms naturally lives or grows

Herbivore animal that eats plants

Heterotrophic organism organism that cannot manufacture its own food; compare *autotrophic organism*

Hydrological cycle biogeochemical cycle that moves and recycles water in various forms through the ecosphere

Hydrosphere water portion of the earth (including water vapor in the air), as distinguished from the solid, gaseous, and living parts

Intrinsic limiting factor factor, such as social stress, that operates within a population to regulate population growth and size; compare *extrinsic limiting factor*

Krill tiny creatures similar to shrimp that live in the ocean and provide food for whales and other sea animals

Landfill a land waste disposal site that is often located without regard to possible pollution of ground-water and surface water due to runoff and leaching; waste is covered intermittently with a layer of earth to reduce scavenger, aesthetic, disease, and air pollution problems

Lichen plants that grow on the surface of rocks and tree bark

Limiting factor factor such as temperature, light, water, or a chemical that limits the existence, growth, abundance, or distribution of an organism

Matter anything that has mass and occupies space

Migration periodic departure and return of individuals to and from an area

Mineral either a chemical element or a chemical compound (combination of chemical elements)

Mutualism a symbiotic relationship between two different species that benefits both species; compare *commensalism, parasitism, symbiosis*

Neritic zone portion of the ocean that includes the estuarine zone and the continental shelf

Niche description of a species' total structural and functional role in an ecosystem

Nitrogen fixation process in which bacteria and other soil microorganisms convert atmospheric nitrogen into nitrates, which become available to growing plants

Nitrogen oxides (NO$_x$) air pollutants that consist primarily of

nitric acid (NO) and nitrogen dioxide (NO$_2$) and oxygen (O$_2$) in air at high temperatures; produced by internal combustion engines and furnaces

Nonrenewable resource resource that can be used up, or depleted to such a degree that further recovery is too expensive; compare *renewable resource*

Nutrient element or compound that is an essential raw material for organism growth and development; examples are carbon, oxygen, nitrogen, phosphorus, and the dissolved solids and gases in water

Oil slick a floating film that is formed atop a body of water by oil that has been spilled into it

Omnivore an animal that can use both plants and other animals as food sources

Overgrazing situation where the grass on an area of land is eaten, usually by too many animals, to the point of damage

Ozone layer layer of gaseous ozone (O$_3$) in the upper atmosphere that protects life on earth by filtering out harmful ultraviolet radiation from the sun

Parasitism a symbiotic relationship between two different species in which one species (the parasite) benefits and the other species (the host) is harmed; compare *commensalism, mutualism, symbiosis*

Perennial a plant whose life span extends over several growing seasons

Pesticide any chemical designed to kill weeds, insects, fungi, rodents, and other organisms that humans consider to be undesirable; examples are chlorinated hydrocarbons, carbonates, and organophosphates

Petroleum (crude oil) dark, greenish-brown, foul-smelling liquid containing a complex mixture of hydrocarbon compounds plus small amounts of oxygen, sulfur, and nitrogen compounds and found in natural underground reservoirs

Photosynthesis complex process that occurs within the cells of green plants whereby sunlight is used to combine carbon dioxide (CO_2) and water (H_2O) to produce oxygen (O_2) and simple sugar or food molecules such as glucose ($C_6H_{12}O_6$)

Plankton microscopic, floating plant and animal organisms in lakes, rivers, and oceans

Pollution undesirable change in the physical, chemical, or biological characteristics of the air, water, or land that can harmfully affect the health, survival, or activities of humans or other living organisms

Population group of individual organisms of the same kind (species)

Population density number of organisms in a particular population per square kilometer or other unit of area

Population distribution variation of population density over a given country, region, or other area

Predation situation in which an organism of one species (the predator) captures and feeds upon an organism of another species (the prey)

Predator organism that lives by killing and eating other organisms

Primary succession ecological succession that begins in an area (such as bare rock, lava, or sand) that has not been previously occupied by a community of organisms

Principle of competitive exclusion no two species in an ecosystem can indefinitely occupy exactly the same niche or exist on the same limited resources

Producer organism that synthesizes its own organic substances from inorganic substances, such as a plant

Rain forests tropical woodlands that grow in hot, humid areas of the earth, near the equator, and receive an annual rainfall of at least 100 inches

Recycle to collect and process a resource so it can be used again, as when used glass bottles are collected, melted down, and made into new glass bottles

Renewable resource resource that potentially cannot be used up; either it comes from an essentially inexhaustible source (such as solar energy from the sun), or it can be renewed by natural or artificially generated cyclical processes so long as it is not used faster than it is renewed; compare to *nonrenewable resource*

Resource (natural) anything needed by an organism, population, or ecosystem; compare also *mineral, nonrenewable resource, renewable resource*

Respiration complex process that occurs in the cells of plants and animals in which food molecules, such as glucose, combine with oxygen and break down into carbon dioxide and water, releasing usable energy

Rodents small, gnawing mammals that include mice, rats, lemmings, beavers, and squirrels, but not rabbits or hares

Runoff lateral movement of nutrients and soil to surface waters

Savanna tropical grassland with grasses and scattered trees

Secondary succession ecological succession that begins in an area (such as abandoned farmland, a new pond, or land disrupted by fire) that had previously been occupied by a community of organisms

Sediment soil particles, sand, and minerals washed from the land into aquatic systems as a result of natural and human activities

Smog originally a combination of fog and smoke; now applied also to the photochemical haze produced by the action of sun and atmosphere on automobile and industrial exhausts

Soil complex mixture of minerals (inorganic compounds), organic compounds, living organisms, air, and water; it is a dynamic body that is always changing in response to climate, vegetation, local topography, parent rock material, age, and human use and abuse

Solar energy direct radiation or energy from the sun plus indirect forms of energy—such as wind, falling or flowing water (hydropower), ocean thermal gradients, and biomass—that are produced when energy from the sun interacts with the earth

Solid waste any unwanted or discarded material that is not a liquid or a gas

Species natural population or group of populations that transmit specific characteristics from parents to offspring; they are reproductively isolated from other populations with which they might breed

Species diversity ratio between the number of species in a community and the number of individuals in each species (for example, low diversity occurs when there are few species but many individuals per species)

Stability persistence of the structure of a system (such as an ecosystem, community, or organism) over time

Succession change in the structure and function of an ecosystem; replacement of one kind of community of organisms with a different community over a period of time; compare *primary succession, secondary succession*

Succulent a plant with thick skin and juicy flesh, capable of storing water

Sulfur dioxide (SO_2) heavy, colorless gas that is very toxic to plants and fairly toxic to humans; it is produced by burning coal and by smelting and other industrial processes

Symbiosis interaction in which two different species live in close physical contact, with one living on or in the other so that one or both species benefit from the association; compare *commensalism, mutualism, parasitism*

Taiga the northern coniferous forest ecosystem

Temperature   the relative hotness or coldness of a substance; it is a measure of the average kinetic energy of all the atoms and molecules in a sample of matter

Territory   area that an organism (such as a lion) will defend against intruders of the same species (other lions)

Topsoil   the rich organic layer of dirt from which plants get nutrients, but which may be washed away by rainwater if left bare and unprotected

Transpiration   direct transfer of water from living plants to the atmosphere

Tundra   the treeless, plains ecosystem of northern arctic regions and high alpine mountaintops

Ultraviolet (UV) radiation   electromagnetic radiation with wavelengths somewhat shorter than those of visible light, but longer than those of X rays; harmful to living things

Water pollution   degradation of a body of water by some substance or condition to such a degree that the water doesn't meet specified purity standards or cannot be used for a specific purpose

Weather   day-to-day variations in atmospheric conditions

Wilderness   area where the earth and its community of life are unaffected by humans and where humans themselves are temporary visitors

Appendix C

Directory of Environmental Organizations

Acid Rain Foundation, Inc.
1410 Varsity Drive
Raleigh, North Carolina 27606

Alliance to Save Energy
1725 K Street, NW #914
Washington, D.C. 20006
(202) 857-0666

America the Beautiful Fund
219 Shoreham Building
Washington, D.C. 20005

American Council for an Energy
   Efficient Economy
1001 Connecticut Ave., NW #535
Washington, D.C. 20036
(202) 429-8873

American Forestry Association
P.O. Box 2000
Washington, D.C. 20010

American Water Works Association
6666 W. Quincy
Denver, Colorado 80235

Animal Welfare Institute
P.O. Box 3650
Washington, D.C. 20007

Audubon Adventures
Route 4
Sharon, Connecticut 06069

California Energy Company
601 California St., Suite 900
San Francisco, California 94108
(415) 391-7700

Californians Against Waste
909 12th Street, Suite 201
Sacramento, California 95814

Canadian Nature Federation
453 Sussex Drive
Ottawa, Ontario K1N 6Z4

Center for Action on Endangered
   Species
175 West Main Street
Ayer, Massachusetts 01432

Center for Environmental
   Information
99 Court Street
Rochester, New York 14604
(716) 546-3796

Center for Marine Conservation
1725 DeSales St., NW
Washington, D.C. 20036
(202) 429-5609

Citizens Clearinghouse for
  Hazardous Waste
P.O. Box 926
Arlington, Virginia 22216
(703) 276-7070

Citizens for a Better Environment
942 Market St., Suite 505
San Francisco, California 94102
(415) 788-0690

Clear Water Action
317 Pennsylvania Ave., SE
Washington, D.C. 20003
(202) 547-1196

Committee for Sustainable
  Agriculture
P.O. Box 1300
Colfax, California 95713
(916) 346-2777

Conservation & Renewable Energy
Inquiry & Referral Service
P.O. Box 8900
Silver Spring, Maryland 20907
(800) 523-2929

Defenders of Wildlife
1244 19th Street, N.W.
Washington, D.C. 20036

Earth Birthday Project
183 Pinehurst, #34
New York, New York 10033

Earth Island Institute
Save the Dolphins
300 Broadway, Suite 28
San Francisco, California
  94133-3312

Ecology Action Centre
1657 Barrington Street, Suite 520
Halifax, Nova Scotia B3J 2A1

Ecology Action of Santa Cruz
P.O. Box 1188
Santa Cruz, California 95061
(408) 476-8088

Energy Probe
100 College Street
Toronto, Ontario M5G 1L5

Environmental Action Coalition
625 Broadway, 2nd Floor
New York, New York 10012

Environmental Action Foundation
1525 New Hampshire Ave., NW
Washington, D.C. 20036
(202) 745-4870

Environmental Defense Fund
257 Park Ave. S
New York, New York 10010
(212) 505-2100

Environmental Hazards
  Management Institute
P.O. Box 932
Durham, New Hampshire 03824
(603) 868-1496

Friends of the Earth
218 D Street, SE
Washington, D.C. 20003
(202) 544-2600

Friends of the Earth
53 Queen Street, Room 16
Ottawa, Ontario K1P 5C5

Geothermal Education Office
664 Hilary Drive
Tiburon, California 94920
(800) 866-4436

Global ReLeaf
The American Forestry Association
P.O. Box 2000
Washington, D.C. 20013

Greenpeace
427 Bloor Street West
Toronto, Ontario M5S 1X7

Greenpeace
1611 Connecticut Avenue, NW
Washington, D.C. 20009

Greenpeace Action
1436 U Street, NW
Washington, D.C. 20009
(202) 462-8817

Household Hazardous Waste Project
901 S. National Ave.
Box 108
Springfield, Missouri 65804
(417) 836-5777

The Humane Society of the United
  States
2100 L Street, NW
Washington, D.C. 20037

Institute for Alternative Agriculture
9200 Edmonston Rd., Suite 117
Greenbelt, Maryland 20770
(301) 441-8777

The Institute for Earth Education
P.O. Box 288
Warrenville, Illinois 60555

Institute for Environmental
  Education
32000 Chagrin Boulevard
Cleveland, Ohio 44124

Institute for Local Self-Reliance
2425 18th Street, NW
Washington, D.C. 20009

The International Crane
  Foundation
E-11376 Shady Lane Road
Baraboo, Wisconsin 53913

The Izaak Walton League of
  America
1401 Wilson Boulevard, Level B
Arlington, Virginia 22209

Keep America Beautiful
9 West Broad Street
Stamford, Connecticut 06892

Long Branch Environmental
  Education Center
Route 2, Box 132
Leichester, New York 28748

National Appropriate Technology
Assistance Service
P.O. Box 2525
Butte, Montana 59702-2525
(800) 428-2525

National Arbor Day Foundation
100 Arbor Avenue
Nebraska City, Nebraska 68410

National Association for the
  Advancement of Humane
  Education
67 Salem Road
East Haddam, Connecticut 06423

National Recycling Coalition
1101 30th Street, NW
Suite 305
Washington, D.C. 20007

National Toxics Campaign
29 Temple Place, 5th Floor
Boston, Massachusetts 02111
(617) 482-1477

Natural Resources Defense Council
122 E 42nd St.
New York, New York 10168
(212) 727-2700

The Nature Conservancy
1815 North Lynn Street
Arlington, Virginia 22209

The New Alchemy Institute
237 Hatchville Road
East Falmouth, Massachusetts
  02536

Renew America
1400 16th St., NW, Suite 710
Washington, D.C. 20036
(202) 232-2252

Rocky Mountain Institute
1739 Snowmass Creek Rd.
Snowmass, Colorado 81654
(303) 927-3128

Society Promoting Environmental
  Conservation
2150 Maple Street
Vancouver, British Columbia V6J
  3T3

Solar Energy Research Institute
1617 Cole Blvd.
Golden, Colorado 80401
(303) 231-7303

StopStyro
2180 Milvia St.
Berkeley, California 94704
(415) 644-6359

Trees for Life
1103 Jefferson Street
Wichita, Kansas 67203

U.S. Fish and Wildlife Service
Publications Unit
130 Arlington Square Building
18th and C Streets, NW
Washington, D.C. 20240

Western Regional Environmental
  Education Council
2820 Echo Way
Sacramento, California 95821

Whale Adoption Project
P.O. Box 388
North Falmouth, Massachusetts
  02556-0388

World Federalist Association
United Nations Office
777 United Nations Plaza
New York, New York 10017

World Resources Institute
1709 New York Ave., NW
Washington, D.C. 20006
(202) 638-6300

World Wildlife Fund
1250 24th St., NW
Washington, D.C. 20037
(202) 293-4800

Worldwatch Institute
1776 Massachusetts Ave., NW
Washington, D.C. 20036
(202) 452-1999

World-Wide Fund for Nature
60 St. Clair Avenue East, Suite 201
Toronto, Ontario M4T 1N5

Index